SOCIOLOGY OF WIDOWHOOD
A STUDY OF VEERASHAIVAS

SOCIOLOGY OF WIDOWHOOD

A STUDY OF VEERASHAIVAS

Vijayalaxmi Biradar

ABHIJEET PUBLICATIONS

DELHI 110094

ABHIJEET PUBLICATIONS
2/46 Tukhmeerpur Extension
Delhi-110 094
Phone: 011-22960492, 65698474
E-mail: abhijeetpublication@gmail.com

SOCIOLOGY OF WIDOWHOOD: A STUDY OF VEERASHAIVAS

First Published 2009

ISBN 978-81-89886-91-2

PRINTED IN INDIA

Published by J.K. Singh for Abhijeet Publications, Delhi-110 094, Lasertypeset by Gaurav Graphics, New Delhi and Printed at Himanshu Printers, Delhi.

GULBARGA UNIVERSITY

Professor B. G. Mulimani

Foreword

Throughout the history of India, Woman has been subjected to inhuman treatment and exploitation. Women constitute nearly half of the world's population, but they have always lagged behind men in getting their rightly deserved share of opportunities in all fields because of the heinous practice of gender discrimination—still prevalent in today's society. In our country many legislations have been brought to protect the rights of women and for their empowerment. Yet the strict implementation of laws has not been possible for various reasons.

Dr. Vijayalaxmi Biradar realizing the need to know more about the woman of India and to understand the many facets of her life, particularly the plight of *widowhood*, which some have to endure, has come out with the present work. It takes a close look at widowhood.

There are a number of works on the problems of widows in Indian Society. The author has chosen to concentrate upon the problems faced by widows of the Veerashaiva Community in Hyderabad Gulbarga Region. The problems faced by widows in the process of their integration within the family, neighbourhood and society at large have been pointed out and the reactions of widows towards their widowhood, widow remarriage and the treatment widows receive among Veerashaivas, in the context of changing socio-economic conditions and life-style have been analyzed. It is noticed that the position of widows within Veerashaiva Community is much better than that in other communities in Indian Society, thanks to the basic liberal tenets of Veerashaiva philosophy. Apart from dealing systematically with the problems faced by Veerashaiva widows, the present work also lays stress on various factors which will lead, eventually, to improvement in their status in the society. The facts and figures presented in the book enhance the importance of the study. Though the study has been, mainly, confined to Veerashaiva Community in the Hyderabad Karnatak Region, it is an unique work and a scholarly exposition of a complex issue touching the core of sentiments of a widow. It is important that the author has drawn attention of the Society, to delve deep into the situation to take all the needed steps, including legislative recommendations, so that the widows lead life with the same dignity as others in the society.

Dr. Vijayalaxmi Biradar deserves a lot of appreciation for this significant contribution on an important issue faced by Indian Society. I am sure the work will serve as a good reference work on the topic.

PROF. B.G. MULIMANI

Preface

In Indian society the women are considered as second class citizens. Generally the traditional Indian Society subordinated the woman and confined her to the home. She had no right of Independent existence. Hence there is a need to know more about the woman in India and to understand the many facets of her life. We have to understand her role as mother, daughter and wife. Apart from this, we come across women who have been deprived of all the privileges and suffered all the time inhuman treatment. To this category belong the widows whose plight is unimaginable in the context of prevailing patriarchal system and double standards of values, one for man and another for woman. Hence this made me to take up an empirical investigation focussing on the problems of integration of Veerashaiva widows in the context of the contemporary Indian society and also studies of widowhood in different communities in India. I had constant discussions with my teachers, intellectuals, social workers and activists, on widow problems that ultimately motivated me to take up the research of which present book is the product.

I undertook research work at the Department of Sociology Gulbarga University, Gulbarga, Karnataka under the supervision and guidance of Dr. L.S. Ainapur, Retd. Professor and Chairman Department of Sociology, to whom I am indebted for invaluable suggestions, academic inspiration and constant encouragement in completing the work. So also I am grateful to Dr. (Smt.) Vinoda Ainapur for her moral support.

It gives great pleasure to extend my sincere thanks to Prof. M.S. Dhadve (Retd.) and Prof. S.L. Hiremath, Department of Sociology, Dean of Faculty of Social Sciences, Gulbarga University, Gulbarga for their kind suggestions and support throughout my work. My thanks are also due to Dr. (Smt.) Nusrath Fatima, Head Department of Studies in Sociology, Dr. Sindhe, Jagannath Reader in Sociology and Dr. Meti Sheshan Reader in Sociology, Gulbarga University, Gulbarga for their cheerful encouragement during my study.

I wish to acknowledge an everlasting depth of gratitude to my loving parents, sisters and brothers for their encouragement and especially to my brother Prof. I Linganagouda S. Biradar, Principal P.D.A. College of Engineering, Gulbarga for his keen interest and constant encouragement in all my academic endeavours. My special thanks are due to my husband Sri Vishwanath Honnalli Advocate for extending all kinds of cooperation in completing this work. I will be failing in my duty if I do not record my gratitude to my children Kumari Sahana and Kumar Adarsh who have also cooperated in completing this work.

I sincerely thank all my respondents, Presidents of Mahila Mandals and Akkanabalagas and Swamijis of Veerashaiva Mathas of Gulbarga for their cooperation during my field work. My thanks are also due to Smt. Annapurna Sajjan, Principal Government College, Gulbarga and to my well wishers and friends for their cheerful encouragement.

Inspite of his hectic schedule Prof. B.G. Mulimani, Vice Chancellor, Gulbarga University, Gulbarga was kind enough to spare his precious time and blessed this book with his candid Foreword. Hence I have indebted to express my sincere thanks to him. I must also thank Mr. J.K. Singh, Prop. of Abhijeet Publications, Delhi, for timely publication of this book.

Dr. Vijayalaxmi Biradar

Contents

Contents

1

Introduction

Woman has been playing a number of traditional roles in her home and has been participating increasingly in various modern tasks due to socio-religious and politico-economic revolutions. She is not only a wife, mother and a house keeper, but also a teacher, an administrator and a politician. She has entered into almost all the fields of human activities. She competes and claims equality with man. But still she has her inadequacies, she lags behind the man as she is tradition-bound and suffers from a number of problems that need urgent attention.

Women constitute about fifty percent of the world population. It is estimated that by A.D. 2000, the total number of women in the world will be more than 3 billion and they will out-number men by nearly 175 million[1].

Throughout the history of India we find that woman is subjected to inhuman treatment. Thus the position, status and role of women in India have been a subject of great concern to women government and the public at large from the beginning. However the plight of women attracted a good deal of attention recently at the international level. Despite enormous efforts, a little has been achieved in bringing about qualitative improvement in the women's development.

As far as the position of woman in Indian society is concerned, it was during the pre-Vedic and Vedic age woman occupied a superior position in society. She has equal rights with man and enjoyed freedom in choosing her life partner. During this period the average woman led a happy and contented life, fondled by her parents, loved by her husband and revered by her children.

Women went to Gurukuls to receive education and married only after acquiring it. A woman was her husband's equal partner and occupied a prominent position in all social and religious ceremonies. In joint family her authority was accepted and she had full liberty of action. Thus according to Alteker "women played a more active economic role and participated in rituals, and girls in higher society were allowed to undergo the Upanayana rite"[2]. The position of mother and wife was an honoured one in the family.

During the post-Vedic age the position of women slowly began to deteriorate. Alteker finds the period from A.D. 500 to A.D. 1800 as one of the progressive deteriorations in the position of women in the Indian society.

Due to the existence of Manu's code of conduct in post-vedic age, the vedic custom of husband and wife jointly taking part in religious functions slowly came to be rejected. Woman's rights depended entirely on her husband and Manu declared that she was not man's equal in her own right. "A husband must be worshipped by a faithful wife as God"[3]. A married woman was not allowed to do anything according to her own pleasures even in her dwelling place. Thus Manu said that "woman is not fit for independence. She has to be always dependent as a child upon the father, as a wife upon the husband, as a widow upon the son"[4].

During this period the introduction of child marriage, rapid decline of female education and consequent growth of illiteracy, prohibition of widow remarriage, the spread of custom of Sati, prevalence of purdah and the growing incidence of polygamous marriages brought about a general decline in the position of women. Women were given the same status as that of Shudras. During the Buddhist period, the status of women was slightly better but from the 8th Century onwards with the foreign invasions, the status of woman again began to fall. When the Britishers began to rule India, the position and status of woman was at the lowest level.

Many stern customs and practices worked against women and left them weak and fragile, and dependent on men from the time of their birth to death. Like this the Indian woman's tale is an endless one of woe and despair. She is abandoned, divorced, bought and sold and killed at the mere whim of man.

Generally the traditional Hindu society subordinated the woman and confined her to the home. The highest duty of woman according to Manu is to obey and serve her husband. She had no right of independent existence. Hence there is a need to know more about the woman of India and to understand the many facets of her life. We have to understand her role as mother, daughter and wife. Apart from this, we come across women who have been deprived of all the privileges and undergo all the time inhuman treatment. To this category belong the widows whose plight is unimaginable in the context of prevailing patriarchal system and double standards of values; one for man and another for woman. Time and again law givers have been depriving the woman of her legitimate roles. In their views the widows have no status and no privileges.

It is only after independence and the promulgation of the Constitution, the intellectuals have been coming forward to undertake research in the social ills.

Though prior to independence the social reformers throughout India struggled against the exploitation of women, children and downtrodden people, tangible results were not expected. In this connection the efforts of Raja Ram Mohun Roy, Ishwarchandra Vidyasagar, Gokhale, Veereshlingam Pantlu, Keshab Chandra Sen, Swami Vivekananda, Bankim Chandra Chatterji, Saratchandra Chatterji, Rabindranath Tagore, Vishnushastri, M.G. Ranade, Eknath, Namadev, Tukaram and others are indeed noteworthy. They highlighted the problems of woman education, abolition of child marriage, widow remarriage and the cruel treatment given to widows. A more comprehensive package of reforms has been brought out by Government of India through passing of several legislations to provide equal opportunities to women and enable them to participate in the national life as equal partners.

There is no aspect of womanhood that has received more sympathy than that of widowhood in India. Because widows are regarded as second class citizens of the country and second class members of their family[5]. Thus, it is very essential to study how a widow integrates herself with the family, neighbourhood, and community even though she is treated as a second class citizen and a second class members of the family devoid of privileges enjoyed by married woman.

It is a regrettable fact that despite the protection accorded to widows' rights by the Widow Marriage Act and the 1954 Hindu Code Bill, there has been no substantial change in the basic position of the widows. Thus widowhood is one of the serious problems faced by the Indian society.

1.1 The Problem

Widowhood is a curse to woman and from ages she has been exploited, humiliated and deprived from decency in living. It is a typical life situation. The age-old prohibition of widow remarriage has had ugly socio-economic consequences. Widowhood brought with it the stigma of impurity for the unfortunate woman, created feelings of moral aversion and distrust towards her, compelling her to lead a life of stern acceticism[6]. In some parts of the country among brahmins, a widow is expected to cut her long tresses, remove all her ornaments, wear only white saris and spend most of her time in some dark corner of the house so that the evidence of her presence be prevented from having an adverse effect on other members of the family. She is shunned and treated as an outcaste and is kept away from places of worship. Nor is she ever included in family rituals, festivals and happy occasions[7].

Unlike spinsters who never had an opportunity to enjoy the protection and security of living with a man, widows suffer agonies that are indeed pathetic. Having had a sheltered life with their husbands, the grief and personal tragedy and the social stigma that they suffer as a consequence of widowhood is enormous[8].

Apart from the social ostracism that is imposed on them the emotional and economic crisis that they undergo in reorganising their lives to have change in the family and social relationships affects their physical and mental health. The severity of grief is greater among young widows who have had a short span of married life and thus have the burden of looking after very young children. This results in an immense emotional and psychological stress, affecting their general status in the family and society and in turn intensifying their social problems.

India under the dictates of tradition had observed child marriage practice and as a result of it, we notice a big gap between husband and wife in age, i.e. 10 to 15 years of difference is being noticed. This, in turn, contributed for the growth of widows population in society. The majority of women are more likely to become widows than to die before their husbands, who are usually older than they. Widowhood is considered a great misfortune. Formerly, and to some extent even today, it was thought to be the result of some sin on the part of the woman, perhaps, committed in previous life.

The condition of the widows varies from society to society indicating their distinctive position, role and status, as prescribed in those particular societies. Sometimes in many societies remarriage is permissible, as in others it is prohibited. But in Veerashaiva community the widow remarriage was not a taboo. They are permitted to go in for another husband.

In Indian society the higher castes prescribed rigid rules for widows and they were not permitted to marry again. Brahmins, Vyshyas, Jains and other castes were very rigid in this respect. It appears that like all high caste Hindus, Veerashaivas found it difficult to bring it into practice owing to their commitment to traditional values of life.

Of course, it is a fact that widowhood brings many changes to the statuses and roles of the affected woman. In fact, the age of a widow has significant role to play. Widowhood at the prime of life is considered to be a curse. It has reflections on her, as if she is the cause of her husband's death and thereby she may be treated as a sinner, and inauspicious personality. 'In a family, her position or fate is certainly in a dilemma, and sometimes derogatory'[9].

The number of widows in our country is on increase. Unfortunately, the widows are regarded as second class citizens or the country and second class members of their families. Even today they are expected to keep away from ornaments, entertainment, good clothes, auspicious functions etc. Above all our society has not changed its concept that a widow must remain a widow always and that she cannot be equated to a married woman.

Barret (1976) expressed the plight of widows by saying that widows belonging to a sub-culture whose members live in despair and loneliness. They chide each other for self pity and advise each other to keep busy. They individually hope for an avenue to escape but collectively succumb to an attitude of hopelessness. The death of the husband is a source of stress requiring more readjustment than any other event in life. The pain of bereavement itself is the first stress that a widow faces. A sense of futility and suspicion that nothing in life is worthwhile, an inability to sleep and a need to blame her fate are found common among the widows[10].

Traditionally, the widow in general had no honourable place in society. Frieda M. Das (1932) opines, "Widows could not remarry, had to renounce their sex, could not pronounce the name of another man, and to live ascetically on fruits, roots and flowers. They had their hair cut, were stripped of jewelry, slept on hard surfaces and had one meal a day. Their presence was unlucky and accused, they were not allowed to join any feasts or merry-making, and they became unpaid drudge. They were easy prey to male relatives, and sometimes escaped by prostitution, suicide or pilgrimages"[11].

Her lot was one of severe hardships and humiliation. There are certain strict religious dictates. Until death she was to observe various vows and fasts. She had to remain chaste and self-controlled and she was not allowed to get remarried, and she is discouraged from taking an active part in any marriage or auspicious ceremony. Even today widows are expected to keep away from ornaments, entertainment, good clothes etc.

Inspite of the fact that studies on women are pouring in during the last few years, studies on widows remain few and far between. A majority of them have devoted on the problem of status of woman, working woman, role, conflicts, problems of adjustment at house and workplaces and problem of inequality. Further these have been to a great extent urban oriented. The double standards prevalent in rural areas in a greater measure kept women under male dominance and servility. It is a rare phenomenon to notice the right place accorded to woman in decision-making process. The problem of girl child is now receiving the attention of sociologists and other social scientists. But there are a few isolated studies available on widowhood and they touch only a fringe of the phenomenon. Again scientific studies on widowhood in different communities in India are lacking. So far we have an image of a widow as it is portrayed in Shastras, Puranas, customs, and proverbs, but hardly have taken steps to examine her status in different significant communities which divorced from the main stream of thought.

There are Jains, Sikhs, Christians, Veerashaivas, Reddis, and a host of other communities and the study of widows in these communities is an urgent task in view of an avowed policy of providing social justice to weaker sections-rarely women in India. It is with this understanding an attempt is made to study the problem of integration of widows in Veerashaiva community which has come to light during the time of Basaveshwara whose movement is a culmination of excessive repression of man and woman through ritualization of life. His thoughts are a protest to the Hindu ritual system and he made it a mission of his life to work for the liberation of man from ritualism and inequality in all fields. The followers of Basaveshwara imbibed his teachings and began to preach for equality and attainment of the highest in spiritual world. Almost 800 years have elapsed since the dawn of this movement and therefore it is contemplated to make a study of widow and her status in Veerashaiva community and thus try to know whether religious ethos and ideas play any significant role in changing the traditional outlook on life. Further, Veerashaiva community lived side by side Hindu community in Karnataka and this fact may compel us to understand how far Veerashaiva community could implement its philosophical ideas in practice and also to assess the extent of impact of traditional ideas on their living. The study purposes to be regional in character and intends to create an awareness among social scientists regarding the need for studying the plight of widows in communities where the rigidity is given up at philosophical level. In this sense it will also be taken as typological in character.

1.2 Main Questions and Objectives of the Study

The position of a widow in society is a crucial topic which sociologists have to discuss and elucidate. The treatment which she receives is often an index to the attitudes of society towards women as a class. The process of integration of widows constitutes the main focus of the study rather than the variety of problems faced by them.

The main questions which the researcher has tried to take up for investigation are as follows:

1. How does a widow integrate herself within the family, neighbourhood and community at large?
2. What are the changes in the socio-economic conditions of Veerashaiva widow?
3. Are there any changes in the life-style of Veerashaiva widows?
4. What are the reactions of widows towards their widowhood?
5. What are the problems faced by widows?
6. What is the position of widow among Veerashaivas?
7. What type of treatment did the widows receive before and after widowhood?
8. What are the views of Veerashaiva widows towards re-marriage, and what are their future plans, suggestions for their welfare?.

The present study is an attempt to understand the process of integration of Veerashaiva widows within family, neighbourhood and community. It takes into, account the various problems faced by Veerashaiva widows, causes and consequences, and efforts made by them to overcome the problems. This study also takes into account the opinions, attitudes of men towards status of Veerashaiva widows. It deals with the factors which improve their status within the society. Hence it pertains to the analysis and position of widows within Veerashaiva community.

1.2.1 Major Objectives of the Present Investigation

1. To study the socio-economic characteristics of respondents just before they became widows and after they became widows.
2. To study the type of family to which they belong and the size of the family, number of working members in the family, property held by them, income enjoyed etc.
3. To ascertain the particulars of the deceased husbands.
4. To know the particulars of widows, including age at widowhood, working status and particulars of their children.
5. To study the attitudes of widows towards remarriage.
6. To know the source of maintenance and support of the widows and their children as also the problems faced by them.
7. To know their plans for their own welfare and welfare of their children.
8. It intended to know the participation of widows in the religious ceremonies and functions arranged by them and by others as also the life style of respondents before and after their widowhood.
9. To examine how the death of a spouse results in major change in household structure.
10. It intends to study the problems of integration of widows among Veerashaivas of Hyderabad Karnataka Region with reference to Gulbarga city.

1.3 Theoretical Perspectives of Integration

The concept of integration is very difficult to define as it is a value loaded term. But most of the social scientists want to define integration in empirical and non-normative terms. However it has been defined variously by sociologists, psychologists and economists. Even within the same discipline the scholars differ in their understanding of the concept of integration.

Sociologists attempted to define social integration in positive non-residual terms. For example Parson conceives integration "as coherence of role and functions in terms of a common or central value system"[12]. Psychologists admit the impossibility of defining it in positive terms. They believe that there are no positive indicators of integration at all. In the society one finds disorganisation in various forms and integration implies "absence of disorganisation"[13]. But economists do not agree with both of these views. They say that once a mans occupation is determined his mode of life and his social status are fixed to a large extent. The harmonious relations of all parts of a social system results in integration. Thus integration is "the fitting together of the parts of a system to constitute a whole".[14]

The concept of integration has been used in many sociological works. The term integration has been used in different contexts by giving different meanings. It has been used by structural-functional analysts and processual analysts, protagonists of conflict school and later by symbolic interactionists.

The concept of integration is used in this work to suit to structural-functional and processual analysis of the phenomenon. It is presumed that family as an institution is integrated with other parts of society.

Integration is a continuous process which takes a long time for a person to integrate within the system. Such a concept we used in our study as a structural-functional thinking. Integration is referred to as a harmonization of all parts of a system. The family is a system which has different parts. These parts must be integrated into the whole. In this system a person takes a lot of time to integrate because it is a continuous process like conflict, co-operation, assimilation etc.

The different sociologists tried to explain the meaning and types of integration in different styles, in different contexts in which they wanted to use it, with the help of their own theoretical perspectives of integration. The integration theory of society is associated with structural-functionalism while it is equally associated with processual analysts and later on with symbolic interactionism. Now we shall try to record the opinion of them individually as well as collectively.

1.3.1 Structural-Functional Perspective

Structural-functional analysis is not new to either the social or the natural sciences. The concepts of structure and function fall into a peculiar set of concepts. Classification of a referent as a function or a structure depends in part on the point of view from which the phenomena concerned are discussed. What is a function from one point of view is a structure from another. For example the concepts of consumption and production are more familiar examples of this peculiar set. The manufacture of automobiles is production from the point of view of an automobile user and consumption from the point of view of a steelmaker. Thus functions in this sense are themselves structures (i.e., patterns) and all structures are the results of operations in terms of other structures (i.e., they are functions). The politeness of small children may be considered as a structure of their behaviour or as a function of operation in terms of the structures (i.e., patterns) of discipline indulged in by their parents. In this connection Francesca M. Cancian stated that the term "functional analysis" or "structural-functionalism" (Merton 1949: Firth 1955) that share only the common element; an interest in relating one part of a society or social system to another part or to some aspects of the whole"[15].

The structural-functional perspective also seeks to delineate the way in which the different structures are coordinated and integrated to preserve the unity of society as a complete system. This approach has contributed significantly to our understanding of many features and customs of society.

According to Alex Inkeles, the basic perspective of the structural-functional point of view, emerges in its prime emphasis on society, and on the interrelations of its institutions, rather than on the individual or groups such as the family. The main question to which it addresses itself is this: 'How is social life maintained and carried forward in time despite the complete turnover in the membership of society with every new generation?' The basic answer it gives is: 'social life persists because societies find means (structures) whereby they fulfil the needs (functions) which are either preconditions or consequences of organized social life'[16].

Structural-functionalism focuses on notions of adaptation, integration and survival[17]. It became enormously popular at the turn of the century. Structural-functionalism involves strands of Pareto, Marshall, Marx, Durkheim, Weber, Radcliffe-Brown, Malinowski, Parsons, Merton, Homans and others. Structural functional perspective became a dominant factor in social thought.

According to J.P. Gillin and J.L. Gillin (1948) "The end result of assimilation and its associated cultural process is integration and sometimes called social unity"[18].

Integration of social group implies organisation, organisation of customs, behaviours, attitudes, interests and sentiments. Integration is organisation, rather than homogeneity. An integrated group is explained in terms of "the degree to which its members, its social categories, statuses and its culture are organised for the achievement of common purposes or goals"[19].

The hallmark of an integrated group is that all the members of the group identify themselves with the group. In it each enjoys a special status and follows patterns of customs without entering into conflict with other customs. Integration involves a degree of reciprocity and equilibrium "a balanced and complementary type of function which rules out homogeneity"[20].

Anthony Giddens and Jonathan H. Turner (1987) have analysed the concept of integration in terms of its three separate dimensions namely 'coordination among social units, the level of symbolic unification among social units and the state of opposition and conflict among social units'[21].

They discussed the basic conditions of social system. They held the view that integration is an essential condition for the survival of a group. The extent to which the compatibility exists between the structural aspects of social system, would decide the level of integration in such societies or systems.

Living of an individual depends on the functional integration of a system. All systems need to be analysed and understood form physical, biological and/or social perspectives. It is said that some unification among parts is essential.

1.3.2 Processual Analysis

Integration is regarded as the process by which internal disputes within a social system are settled without the degree of opposition and conflict among social units.

Merton (1967) treated integration as a formal concept. To him norms are integrative elements in a society. He considered them as strict demanding obedience from the members persistence of relations has been accepted as a very important condition which ensures integration. Parsons agreed with Merton on this necessary condition of society.

Parsons visualised integration in the interrelationship of its component parts. He regarded integration as a process by which "relations to the environment are mediated in such a way that the distinctive internal properties and boundaries of the system and entity are maintained in the face of variability in the external situation"[22].

For Parsons social system is self sustaining phenomenon. This is achieved through various mechanisms that strike a balance between need dispositions and means to achieve them. It maintains its own boundary and is found distinct from other systems. His view is that individuals are motivated and oriented towards realization of cultural goals by respecting the norms and showing a greater attachment to them. He is guided by social norms which have been internalised by him. He believed in the institutional integration of actions and elements. Analysis of the concept of integration to parsons has a double reference. Integration presupposes an orderly process of change of the system.

The concept of double reference is stated in terms of "*(a)* to the compatibility of the components of the system with each other, so that change is not necessitated before equilibrium can be reached, and *(b)* to the maintenance of conditions of distinctiveness of the system within its boundaries against its environment"[23].

MacIver and Page (1955) have regarded integration as a process in which the differences between the members of society are harmonised instead of being suppressed or compromised.

T.A. Cuttat (1963) has considered integration as a process of becoming whole. Further it was felt that integration process is a continuous one and is directed towards becoming a whole.

Mair (1970) described integration as "an integrated society is one in which established institutions and rights and values associated with them are generally accepted"[24].

Still there are others who define integration as a central value system. "They hold the view that integration is revolving around a set of fundamental values accepted by a large number of persons in a society".[25]

The typical functionalist approach to the concept of integration is to equate it with lack of conflict. Four kinds of definitions in terms of absence of conflict can be distinguished.

- "The first defines integration as logical meaningful consistency among social patterns (Sorokin 1962, Vol. 1, pp. 15, 23). Integration means that similar themes, values or principles are used in all spheres of social life.
- The second definition of integration focuses on the absence of aggression and exploitation of the powerless among members of a social system. An integrated system is marked by co-operation, consensus on mutual rights and duties, and loyalties that crosscut the subgroups within the system.
- The third definition focuses on the absence of conflicting demands on individuals as to the appropriate behaviour or feelings in a specific situation.
- The fourth definition concerns the fit between individual's motivation and the behaviour required by the social system"[26].

Widowhood is considered as a social category within the society. It is a particular position or status or social stigma attached to a woman after the death of her husband. It is quite natural that a woman is disintegrated when she loses her husband. Whatever caste or religion it may be we find that a widow feels lonely, loss of security, alone, aloof after his death. But this feeling appears as a temporary phenomenon. She will again reintegrate to her normal life or mainstream of life after few days. This process of reintegration is treated in this work as integration process. Society has a number of mechanisms through which she starts to integrate with the members of her family, kiths and kins. For instance joint family serves as a mechanism for a widow in her process of integration. If she happens to be the head of the family, she has to bear the burden of maintaining family affairs. Through the guidance of elders she gets a new role. In this new role she keeps herself busy and begins to forget the unhappy incident. Thus the process of integration begins to operate.

As she becomes aged she plays a very respectable role as a grandmother, mother-in-law. These roles make her free from stigma of widowhood. Even others also invite her in all activities. Gradually she forgets the stigma of widowhood as she commands the respect from the members of the family and community.

The theoretical models adopted in this study helps in understanding the process of integration. Structural functional model is treated as much suitable for such a study.

1.4 Review of Literature

Although there is no dearth of sociological and anthropological studies on women in different societies, the sociological studies on women in particular community are limited. Recently a few studies have referred to Veerashaiva women and their participation in social life. Apart from making certain casual remarks on Veerashaiva widows a full-fledged sociological study on Veerashaiva women is very rare. A few studies have highlighted the atrocities committed to widows and analysed the changes in their status and role. Integration of widows into family, neighbourhood and community has not been a theme chosen for search. Again the Veerashaiva widows of Hyderabad-Karnataka region did not receive any attention. To fill this gap, the present work has been undertaken.

We can roughly divide the studies concerning women into two categories based on their nature and content:

I. Studies on women in general.

II. Studies on widows in particular.

I. Of late literature on the life of women in society has been brought out by scholars in social science, and humanities. It is a difficult task to mention all the works on women. However, an attempt is made to record the findings of a few important representative works. The studies so far carried out have included tribal, rural as well as urban women.

In the first category we include the studies on women in general. These studies have dealt with the social, economic, religious and cultural life of women living in different parts of the country. The effects of the various processes such as modernization, urbanization, westernization and industrialization have been examined with reference to religion, family, marriage and the status of women in general. The works of M. N. Srinivas (1976), S. K. Ghosh (1989) on 'Indian Women Through the Ages', Sushma Sood (1990), Sushila Agarwal (1988), Pramila Dandvate, Ranjana Kumari and Jamila Verghese (1989), C. Raghunandha Reddy (1986), Neera Desai and Vibhuti Patel (1985), R. K. Sapru (1989), Leelamma Devasia and V. V. Devasia (1990), Neera Desai (1977), Chandrashekhar S. (1968), Menon, Lakshmi N. (1975), Bose, A. (1975), Sheikh M. H. Kidwai (1978), R. K. Saxena (1978), Alfred D'Souza (1980), Mumtaz Ali Khan (1982), Dr. Sushila Mehta (1982), Indira (1987), Tafari and Nahid Yagnesh (1982), Manindra Kapoor (1987), Giddumal Dayaram (1989), A. S. Altekar (1987), Rekhadevi Raju (1988), Sachchidananda Ramesh P. Sinha (1984), Leela Mullatti (1989) are very significant. The major findings of these studies are attempted in the following pages.

M.N. Srinivas (1976) in a survey of the changing position of Indian women points out that there has been a rapidly increasing concern both with the role and position of women specially after the second world war. The processes of modernization, westernization and industrialization have brought about a greater equality between the sexes than before. Infact urban women have taken a very bold step to greater equality with men in every field. But village women and tribal women are still lagging behind. He further goes on to say "that until very recently, too much attention has been paid to the legal, theoretical and formal dimensions of women's position, and too little to actual relations between men and women, and their dynamic relation over a period of time (1976)"[27].

The book *Sociological Essays on Veerashaivism* (1972) of C. Parvathamma is a collection of essays which were published in different professional journals. She put these essays together in this volume without any extensive changes in original papers to become easy for readers.

This volume highlights some aspects of Veerashaivism in relation to caste structure, notions of purity, pollution, the economic drive and the liberal philosophy behind all these. It also throws light on political aspirations of the Veerashaiva community in Mysore state. In this connection the author states that "the sectarian religious movement today has crystalised itself into a large number of occupational groups which sometime cut-across and at other times unite against other caste groups depending upon the interests involved"[28].

Sheikh M.H. Kidwai (1978) in his study 'Woman Under Different Social and Religious Laws', explained the changing conditions of women in general. This particular work is a fascinating study and will prove a boon to historians, sociologists and others who are curious to know the status of women folk. In this volume the author has highlighted the status and legal rights of the women in different important religions of the world, namely, Buddhism, Judaism, Christianity and Islam.

Ramanamma (1979) studied the graduate women in

an urban setting (Poona city). She stated that in many traditional countries including ours "women are treated as mere chattels with no freedom of movement, speech and action, and are controlled by their men. In the typical traditional patriarchal joint family the head of the family, who is invariably a male, rules it like a monarch. The personality system is subordinated to structural system of the joint family"[29]. She has examined the status of rural woman. She is convinced over the fact that except the head of the family all others are subordinates and dependent. The position of women is still worst. A woman with a male child may receive some good treatment. Her role as mother is complimented.

Sushila Mehta (1982) in her study on 'Revolution and the Status of Women in India' says that, "as far as traditions and cultural values are concerned no independent status for women has been recognised by traditional Indian society. And her expression about woman and her roles are important in so far as they are complementary to man. A woman in traditional Hindu society had no independent existence. She had no rights as a citizen in her own independent status"[30].

She held the view that women's roles and their rights and duties are related to men. The social system has developed certain mechanisms through which the traditions are preserved. The changes in the traditional patterns of living are very slow due to the process of acculturation. She advocated for revolutionary changes in the status of woman so that she can be independent and enjoy the rights and privileges like others.

Neera Desai and Vibhuti Patel (1985) in their work 'Indian Women: Change and Challenge', aimed at examining the impact of International Women's Decade (declared by United Nations in 1975) on the lives, status and struggles of women in India. In their analysis, aspects of Indian women are highlighted in the context of changing socio-economic and political reality of the Indian subcontinent. They also made an attempt to answer some of the vital questions affecting women.

C. Raghunadha Reddy (1986) in his work 'Changing Status of Educated Working Women' made an attempt to know the attitudes, opinions and behavioural patterns of educated working women in India. He has stated very clearly the attitudes of working women towards marriage, family, education, etc., and how working women (office staff, teaching staff and medical staff) differ among one another with regard to age at marriage, selection of marriage partner, attitude towards love marriage, intercaste marriage, dowry, divorce, relations with in-laws, decision making, the importance of sex in married life etc. He made a comparative study of pre- and post-independence Indian women. He analysed the plight of women before the pre-independence days and the glory enjoyed by the modern women.

Sushila Agarwal (1988) in her cross-cultural study on 'Status of Women' made an attempt to understand the changing status of women in India and Canada with special reference to social, legal and educational aspects. She tried to argue that unless constitutional and legal provisions are interpreted from social perspective, they can not deliver the desired results.

It also seeks to analyse the role of educational counsellors in raising consciousness and in providing girls and boys skills to effect change in perceptions about the roles of men and women in society.

Rekhadevi Raju (1988) in her work on 'Status of Women', made a comparative study of rural and tribal women living in close proximity. She did a cross cultural study in anthropological perspective. She also attempted to analyse the status of women on the basis of their roles as daughter, daughter-in-law, sister-in-law, mother, mother-in-law and widow. While discussing the problems of widow remarriage she argues that in tribal communities there are fewer restrictions as compared to rural communities.

The social situation in rural area appears to be hostile to widow remarriage.

Leela Mullatti (1989) in her work on the 'Bhakti Movement and the Status of Women', attempted to analyse the impact of protest (Bhakti) movements on the status of women in India. She states that, the protest movements aimed at doing away with the manifold taboos, pollutions and rituals with which Hindu religion was cluttered. Some of them have accepted the equality of men and women, while others reinforced the inequalities in practices.

Her study is based on case study of Veerashaivism, a populous sect in Karnataka. She deals with the impact of this movement on the status of women. Her contention that precepts and practices meet in a unique way among Veerashaivas needs to be studied scientifically. Child training practices the institution of marriage, the family and kinship system and the economic and socio-religious life of Veerashaiva women enable them to enjoy a comparatively high status.

S.K. Ghosh (1989) in his book *Indian Women Through the Ages* surveyed the history and vicissitudes of the status and condition of women in the course of long history of Indian civilization. In this work the author saw how the position, power, status and disabilities of the daughter, the wife and the widow went on changing in course of time in all communities—Hindus, Muslims, Christians, Sikhs, Parsis and tribals who form the strength of our society. Women once enjoyed considerable freedom and privileges in the spheres of family, religion and public life. But as centuries rolled by, the situation went on changing adversely for them.

Ghosh maintained that the introduction of child marriage, rapid decline of female education and consequent growth of illiteracy, prohibition of widow remarriage, the spread of the custom of sati, prevalence of purdah and the growing incidence of polygamous marriages brought about a general decline in the position of women. He stated that "many stern customs and practices worked against women and left them dependent from the time of their birth to the time of their death"[31]. He discussed at length the disabilities and deprivation of women as wife and widow. Their exploitation created problems of security at home, workplace and street. About widows he stated that most of them have taken to the life of a prostitute undergoing economic crises and mental torture. Divorced and separated women are in no way better off than the other categories of deprived women.

In his study he highlighted the efforts made by eminent social reformers—Raja Ram-Mohan Roy, Ishwarchandra Vidyasagar, Keshab Chandra Sen, Swami Vivekanand, Bankim Chandra Chatterji, Sarat Chandra Chatterji, Rabindra Nath Tagore, Vishnu Sastri, M.G. Rande, Eknath, Namdev, Tukaram—to improve the conditions of women. After independence woman's liberation movement took up the cause of women in order to remove disabilities of women in all walks of life.

Several laws have been enacted bringing about changes at various levels—within home, family, workplace and in the streets. These laws have improved their status in society.

'Women and Development' (1989) of R.K. Sapru is a collection of research papers and articles. These papers and articles are a multidisciplinary investigations into various aspects of pressing socio-economic problems facing women in India. It also made a comprehensive evaluation of the status of women in the world today and its future taking into account socio-economic development as well as scientific and other factors.

'Violence Against Women' (1990) of Sushma Sood is a collection of articles which aim at examining various atrocities against women like bride burning, wife battering, compelling to become sati, depriving widows from normal life, domestic violence, female infanticide, foeticide and also the violence against the elderly females.

The several articles edited in this volume offered certain practical suggestions to overcome the tragic life of women in society.

'Women in India: Equality Social Justice and Development' (1990) edited by Leelamma Devasia and V. V. Devasia presents discerning articles by different authors on various concerns on the improvement of women. They explained the process of achieving equality through education and employment. The social and economic development of Dalit and tribal women through forestry and other income-generating programmes has been recorded. A few articles are devoted to the status of Muslim women in the context of Quranic injunctions. Also in one of the articles, the theme of women entrepreneurship is highlighted.

A. Suryakumari (1990) in her article 'Women in India: Beyond Inequality and Exploitation', analysed the inequal position and exploitation of women in India. The author opines that the inequality and exploitation of women originated in the later Vedic period. This inequality and exploitation imposed on women have to be seen in the total content of a society where large sections of the population, male and female, adults and children suffer under the oppression of an exploitative system. Further he states that this system of exploitation of women in India, differs from rural to urban. The author concludes that, comparing to men, Indian women have lower status within the society. Not only this, even the Indian social system narrowed options for women for their development. The differential distribution of power between the sexes is considered as a major obstacle in the pursuit of equality.

In the light of above discussion, it becomes somewhat easy to interpret the past and present position of women within the society.

II. Although the problems of widows have been highlighted by the social reformers as early as 19th century, scientific studies dealing with the problems of widows in different social setting were undertaken only during the past three decades. Sociologists, social anthropologists and students of literature have shown a great concern for the rehabilitation and integration of widows. The following works clearly explain the attempts made by scholars in this direction. These can be categorised into the following areas of study.

a) Widows in historical perspective.

b) Social and economic conditions of working and non-working widows.

c) Problems, issues, strategies and rehabilitation of widows.

d) Widows in rural and urban areas.

e) Regional and community-wise studies of widows.

f) Aged widows.

g) Deprivation and atrocities as women through traditional means.

Studies on widows in historical perspective were undertaken by Krishnakumari, N.S. (1987), Saroj Gulati (1985), Jogeshchandra Ghosh and Ila Mukherjee. Krishnakumari in her work on status of single woman in India, tried to explain the status of single woman as a widow, divorcee and spinster. She states the single woman today is asserting her right as individual in all walks of life. But this is not true in case of Indian woman. In Indian context she has to wage a losing battle against the existing social norms and prejudices. She has discussed three categories of women namely spinsters, widows and divorced. She comes to conclusion that there is hardly any difference in the intensity of their problems. They share the same experience.

Ila Mukherjee in his work on social status of north Indian women (1526-1707 AD), highlighted the pitiable position of widows. He explained in detail the position of widow from Vedic period to Mughal period. In this context he discusses the dishonourable position of widows, the practice of Sati and widow remarriage. Regarding the position of widows, the author opines that, "the condition and status of widow changed substantially from the early period to the period under review. A widow was treated very inhumanly by the members of her family. Her life was restricted by numerous social taboos. Her very appearance was considered inauspicious on occasions like birth, marriage, etc. The death of a man deprived his wife of all her worldly pleasures, till the Vedic period. The Vedic literature permitted the custom of Niyoga and the remarriage of widows. Even the remarriage of widows was considered as a matter of great dishonour and infidelity in Hindu society"[32].

A few works described the socio-economic background of widows were undertaken by Nagesh, H.V. and Katti, A.P. (1984), Ken and Zick (1986), D. Radhadevi (1988) and Raja Ratnam and Gandhi (1988). They tried to know their socio-economic conditions and problems of widows. In these studies, it is said that the widows face problems of all levels. Nagesh and Katti have stressed on the deprivation of women in respect of using facilities in life. In their study on 'A socio-economic study of widows in northern Karnataka', they opine that widowhood is a status of deprivation of economic, social and psychological. Religion, Myths and the practices like Sati have made it more difficult to consider it in a rational and humanistic way. In their study, they studied the socio-economic characteristics of widows, particulars of the deceased husbands, the source of maintenance and support of the widows and their children, problems of widows like food, shelter, clothing, education, etc., attitudes of widows towards remarriage and their future plans. Their study includes the widows from both Hindus and Lingayat community. It was revealed that some of the widows at least were reluctant for remarriage for want of societal approval.

Ken R. Smith and Cathleen D. Zick (1986) in their article on 'The incidence of poverty among the recently widowed: mediating factors in the life course', have analysed the factors influencing the economic effects on widowhood. They have made use of six variables viz., income, the calendar year of widowhood, age at widowhood, sex, years of marriage and past work experience. They treated them as mediating factors. They reactedly had the conclusion that survivors with many years of work experience have lower incidence rates of poverty than those who have little or no prior labour market experience.

D. Radhadevi (1988) in her study on "work participation of widows in India", deals with the economic implications of widowhood and its interaction with emotional aspects. Her study of the phenomenon revolves round the three hypotheses related to widows work participation. They are

1. "Widows will face more economic strain and their work participation rate will be much higher than that of their married peers.
2. The proportion of widow workers will be higher in occupations with least difficulties for entry.
3. The third hypothesis relates to the length of active work participation"[33].

The results of her study show that the widows in urban area undergo a greater strain and are required to work more; a large number of widows accept the occupations where entry is easy and are in a position to work for a longer period as evidenced by several other workers.

T Rajaratnam and E. Gandhi (1988) in their study on "socio-economic and demographic aspects of widowhood in Tamil Nadu", analysed the problems of widowhood at young age. It is found associated with marriage at tender age, and higher age difference between husband and wife, and by their poor socio-economic status. They suggest that, such policies must be formulated which would help to narrow down the husband-wife age difference and improve overall socio-economic status of women including raising the age at marriage of both males and females. They further opine that the condition of widows and widowers is very poor which requires implementation of more social and economic security schemes for their upliftment.

A few works describing the problems, issues and strategies for rehabilitation of widows have been undertaken by Bhagwant Rao Dubey (1964), Ch. Muthyalayya Naidu (1965), Rama Mehta (1970), S.N. Agarwala (1967), Mumtaz Ali Khan and Noor Aysha (1982), Lopamudra (1983), C. Raghunandha Reddy (1986), Aradhya B.M.M. (1987), Gurmeet M.P. Singh and Sukhdeep Gill (1986), Ainapur L.S. (1987), M.P. Singh (1988), H.V. Nagesh, R.S. Nair and Katti A.R. (1988) and Cathleen D. Zick and Ken. R. Smith. In these studies it is said that the remarriage of widows is a social problem, which creates various problems in the life of widows, and as a strategy it has proved successful in certain regions of India.

Bhagwant Rao Dubey (1964) made a study on "Widow remarriage in Madhya Pradesh". His study is based on field-work in three villages of Madhya Pradesh, which includes three castes, viz., Rajput, Kulmis and Balais in the Narbada valley in Madhya Pradesh. His work highlighted the fact that nearly 40% widows have been rehabilitated through remarriage. The factors forming remarriage have been explained. To him widow remarriage is not only an urban phenomenon but also is practiced in rural areas.

Ch. Muthyalayya Naidu's (1965) "Beginnings of widow remarriage movement in India" deals with the origin and spread of widow remarriage movement in India. He says that the widow remarriage was started by Ishwarchandra Vidyasagar for the first time in 1864, and later on it was continued by his followers. It was also favoured by British

Government by passing the civil marriage act in 1911.

Rama Mehta (1970) in her work on "The western educated Hindu women", discussed widow remarriage as a social problem. She opines that widow remarriage is possible only when the widows could establish a life for themselves and be accepted without undue attention. She further states that the problem of widow remarriage is not an isolated problem, it was intimately connected with the whole fabric of society. As that fabric changed its complexion, automatically the position of widows also improved.

S.N. Agarwala (1967) in his article on "widow remarriages in some rural areas of northern India", opines that widows belonging to high-caste Hindus in India do not remarry due to various social restrictions imposed on their remarriage. A study carried out by the author, in Mathura and Saharanpur districts in Uttar Pradesh and in Rohtak district in Punjab has brought out that nearly 30% of the widowed are remarried. His survey covered 6,211 households, of which 887 were Muslim and the remaining were Hindus. He obtained the standardized widow remarriage rates to find out whether differences in widow remarriage percentages by district were real or were due to variations in the distribution of the ever widowed females by age, occupation, caste and the number of living children. The author states that as a result of standardization for age, number of living children and caste, the difference in widow remarriage rate narrowed down considerably. In his study Brahmanic influence is regarded as a major factor for lower percentage of widow remarriage.

He further considers that, widow remarriages were found to be very common among younger and childless widows and highest among Muslims and lower castes among Hindus. The reason for this is that, they have social approval of remarriages. But among other high caste Hindus, such as Brahmins, Banias, Khatris, the cases of widow remarriage were very few, because of a long standing religious sanctions against such remarriages.

Mumtaz Ali Khan, Noor Aysha (1982) in their study on the 'Status of Rural Women in India' made an attempt to discuss widow marriage. The authors opine that the position of the widow depends on several considerations of which the social values and attitudes form the most important base. Widows in Hindu society had been subjected to severe restrictions, sanctions, prohibitions and taboos. Even a young widow was not free from these disabilities.

They further stated that widow marriage was practically an impossibility among the Hindus in the past. Since 1955 the Hindu law permits marriage of widows. We notice the occurrence of widow marriage instances. The rule appears to be rigid in the case of higher caste Hindus and not in the case of lower castes.

Lopamudra (1983) in her article "The Plight of Widows" states that despite the protection accorded to women's rights by the Widow Remarriage Act and the 1954 Hindu Code Bill, widows still remain second class members of both the family and the society. Even today they are discouraged from taking an active part in marriage or any auspicious ceremony. She advocates adult education programme for widows and pleads for the establishment of Vocational centres where they may work and become self-dependent. She has pleaded for providing hostel facilities for single woman.

B.M.M. Aradhya (1987) in his article "what it means to be a widow" states "shocked, stunned and immobilised, the widow finds it extremely difficult to pierce the gloom that envelops her life". In his discussion he has dealt with the causes of widowhood, social stigma and taboos attached to widows and overwhelming depression of widows. Lastly he opines that only education, economic protection, legislation and changing the attitude of society towards the widowhood would certainly improve the position of widows. Education and employment if not remarriage are the only way to remove the hardships of widows.

Gurmeet M.P. Singh and Sukhdeep Gill (1986) in their article 'problems of widowhood' made an exploratory study of 140 widows from Ludhiana city to identify their problems regarding money, child-rearing and social life. They found that widows have faced the problems of bringing up of their children, economic hardships, maintenance of social give-and-take relations.

Dr. L.S. Ainapur (1987) in his essay on "strategies to overcome the problems of widows", categorised the widows into different groups viz., widows after their sixties, child widows, widows who have one or two children, educated widows and employed widows. He suggested some strategies and measures to overcome the problems of widows. To overcome the problems of widows it is regarded as essential to conduct the scientific surveys and investigations in order to know the multidimensional character of the phenomenon. Education, remarriage of the child and childless widows, economic independence of women, programmes emphasising the need for change in the attitudes of people towards widows etc. are suggested. He advocated the increasing role of voluntary organizations in taking-up programmes for the welfare of widows. Also the political parties should undertake the rehabilitation programmes to improve the living conditions of widows.

Gurmeet M.P. Singh (1988) in his article on "Restraints to widow remarriage" made a survey of 140 widows from Ludhiana city between the age of 25 years to 70 years, to explore the restraints which came into the way of remarriage of widows. The main objectives of his study are: *i)* to identify the restraints to widow remarriage, *ii)* to identify the age differences in restraints to widow remarriage, *iii)* to identify the differences in restraints faced by working and non-working widows.

The author states that by analysing the data four major restraints to widow remarriage were emerged. Among them the most frequently cited restraint was love and respect for the husband. Other restraints are concerned to children's welfare, disrespect by society and too old children.

H.V. Nagesh, P.S. Nair and A.P. Katti (1988) in their book "widowhood in India", discussed profiles of widows in India, problems and issues of widowhood, community attitudes and perceptions, policies and programmes of widow rehabilitation.

This volume is a collection of seminar papers. It has three parts, the first part of the book deals with the magnitudes and prospects of widowhood in near future. The authors state that "the incidence of widowhood in the early and adulthood ages has declined in India over time, the absolute figures of widows are on the increase. Further, as a consequence of population aging coupled with favourable morbidity conditions for aged females, there is a prospect of increasing incidence of widowhood in old ages (60+)"[34].

The second part of the volume deals with issues and perspectives. It begins with how the cultural ideology of Hindus is maintained in crisis like widowhood. Three papers deal with the state of deprivation and the adjustment problems of widows. A few papers surveyed the perception and practice of widowhood in five religions viz., Hindu, Christian, Islam, Jain and Lingayat.

The third part of the volume deals with policies and programmes of rehabilitation of widows in India. One paper of the volume deals with the efforts made during the last few years for rehabilitation of widow in India in general and Maharastra in particular.

"Widows Abandoned and Destitute Women in India" (1989) of Pramila Dandvate, Ranjana Kumari and Jamila Verghese, focuses on the socio-economic, religious and cultural aspects of the status of widows, abandoned and destitute women in India.

This book discussed the development of women's rights through the centuries and analysed the torture and harassment inflicted on dowry victims and Devadasi system. The findings of this work are based on a study of the widows of Varanasi. It makes a survey of the measures adopted to improve the conditions of widows. This volume further makes a social audit of the legislation. The shortcomings in the implementation of the programmes are analysed. Political will is considered as very important to solve the problems of women, in general and problems of widows in particular.

Neera Desai and M. Krishnaraj (1990) in their work *Women and Society in India,* discussed widow remarriage and problems faced by widows. While discussing regarding widow remarriage they state that there are some permissible conditions for widow remarriage in some communities (e.g. levirate marriages). They also hold an idea that, the practice of widow remarriage was shunned by the upper caste Hindus as well as by the elites among other religious groups. As for the problems of widows are concerned they opined that, widows are facing a social, religious, food and clothing problems. But on the other hand they view that the self-immolation by a widow was an act of highest merit. Even today many villages worship the site where a 'sati' was committed. They advanced certain suggestions for the rehabilitation of widows. They are: *i)* helping the widows to be economically independent and law should protect their rights, *ii)* A concerted effort towards social education is needed for attitudinal change towards widows, and *iii)* A new laws were put for widow's right to share in the husband's property.

Cathleen D. Zick and Ken R. Smith in their study on "Recent Widowhood, Remarriage and Changes in Economic Well being", examine changes in family composition due to the death of a spouse, and subsequent remarriage, affecting her economic status. It is observed that the widow remarriage measure has brought economic gains to the widow. On the other hand the widows who do not remarry remain economically handicapped. The economic status of a widow differs to a greater extent from that of a married widow.

G.S. Bidarakoppa (1971) in his article on "Position and Problems of Hindu Widows", tries to explain the position and economic, family, social, health and emotional problems of widows. He also attempted to analyse some of the acts that were passed by the Government for the welfare of widow. Even though the efforts made by the Government and voluntary organizations the widow still encounters difficulties due to many social and psychological forces.

Apart from these there are a few other studies which describe the status of widows in rural and urban communities. The works of A.B. Bose and M.L.A. Sen (1965), T.N. Kitchlu (1979), Rekha Mehra, K. Saradamani (1983), Lokesh Chandra Nand (1989), Rekha Bhagat and P.N. Mathur (1989), Shyama Lal (1971) are noteworthy.

It is observed that the stress and strain of widows persisted in rural as well as urban communities. There appears to be no significant change in the position of widows in rural and urban areas. They have described the age composition of widows and their economic status was analysed. They speak of the insecurity that a widow undergoes and face numerous problems, and make a plea for providing security to widows. In a Brahmin village of Palghat the widows make their own living and thus do not depend on others. Widows are forced to lead a simple life. The orthodox section of the population retained the rigid attitude towards widows. Rekha Bhagat and P.N. Mathur held the view that widow remarriage provides an opportunity to resettle in the society and thus make herself free from the curse of widowhood.

There are a few studies which are regional in nature.

The works of Dr. C. Harichandran (1982), Mrs. Marcus B Fuller (1900) and J. Henry Korson (1975), Baidyanath Saraswathi (1983) are very significant. These have been conducted in the different parts of India. They help in providing a better perspective of the situation. They dealt with the socio-economic conditions of widows. They discussed the logic of permanent widowhood. The Kashiwasi widows' study revealed the ideological structure of the widowhood in traditional India. They emphasised the conditions of Hindu widows and very little attention is paid to widows in Muslim and Christian communities.

Of late sociologists have dealt with the aged widows. Dr. Samita Manna's (1991) study is very much relevant for understanding the practices a widow can undertake in her old age. She made a study of aged widows of Bengal. Her study is mainly divided into three sections. In the first section she related the position of widows from Vedic period to 19th century. In her second section, she discussed the familial background and demographic characteristics of 70 aged widows of Naihati, an urban town of the West Bengal. The third section of her study deals with the restrictions like wearing dress, intaking of food and observing Bar and Bratas etc., and their effect on their action, pattern and ways of life. She argued that the caste has a distinctive role in this matter, higher the caste, greater the restrictions and lower the caste, less the restrictions. These restrictions are automatically come down on them through scriptural behests, and these are conventionally followed.

Godavari Patil (1989) in her work on "Hindu widows: A study of deprivation" examined the state of deprivation among Hindu widows of Dharwad district. She has treated caste, age, income, area and education as independent variables, property left by the husband as infrastructure variable and deprivation as dependent variable for the analysis of the data, related to rural and urban Hindu widows of Dharwad district. The major conclusions of her study are: comparing to rural widows, the mean duration of widowed life of urban widows is low, and greater number of urban widows started working after becoming widows. And most of the rural and urban widows wish to live with their children. With regard to the age at death of the deceased husbands, her study reveals that there is no significant difference between urban and rural area.

One of the most significant findings of her study is that, a majority of the widows faced difficulties in controlling their children due to the absence of the male member at home. She further concludes that both urban and rural widows irrespective of their castes have faced economic problems. Widows belonging to different age groups, young and middle aged widows have faced more economic problems than the aged widows. With regard to social deprivation faced by the widows she concludes that both urban and rural widows have faced greater social deprivation after widowhood than before. Thus the state of social deprivation differs from caste to caste, from different age groups, even there is a decrease in the frequency of kinsmen's visits to widows after their widowhood. Not only this even they face an emotional and cultural deprivation.

Her study indicates that intermediate agencies should develop to train the widows educationally and vocationally to find a suitable employment and to ensure social security. It is evident from her study that widow's disapproval of remarriage is due to lack of religious and social sanction for remarriage. The study also indicates need for more social participation by widows in order to reduce their general dissatisfaction in life.

The brief review of literature attempted above on widows shows the wide ranging aspects concerning the study of widows in time and space. These studies either have dealt with the different aspects of life of widows in general or have made an attempt to examine one or two aspects of the living of widows in a particular community. The caste, racial and regional differences are so obvious that any single study will not provide an all India picture of the position of the widows. However, detailed and careful studies concerning the social, economic and integrational aspects of widows in particular community are few and far between. Moreover, there is no work particularly referring to Veerashaiva widows of Hyderabad-Karnataka, apart from some passing references to the position of Veerashaiva widows in some monographs and occasional chapters devoted in text books of sociology.

In this context, it was felt appropriate to carry out detailed study of Veerashaiva widows, their problems and integrational perspectives and to bridge this gap in our knowledge the present study is undertaken.

1.5 Operational Definitions

- *Integration:* In the present work, reintegrating to normal life or main stream of life is considered as integration process, or behaviour, as of an individual, that is in harmony with the environment.
- *Widow:* A woman who has lost her husband by death and has not married again is known as a widow.
- *Widower:* A man whose wife is dead and who has not married again is known as a widower.
- *Widowhood:* State of being a widow is widowhood.
- *Family:* It is defined as a group of persons living together, taking food from the same kitchen and related by blood, marriage or adoption (census, 1961).
- *Nuclear family:* It consists of the married couple and their children.
- *Joint family:* It consists of more than three generations who live together in the same household. All the

men are related by blood and the women of the household are their wives. Unmarried girls and widows of the family are kinsmen.

- *Veerashaiva:* A brave person who is engaged in seeking Linganga Samarasya, is a Veerashaiva.
- *Community:* A group of people living in definite geographical area having a sense of feeling of oneness is known as a community.
- *Neighbourhood:* The place where different families live is known as a neighbourhood.
- *Widow-pensioner:* One who receives widow pension, which is given to the person whose husband is dead and is a destitute is a widow-pensioner.

1.6 Methodology

A systematic sociological study on Veerashaiva widows in Hyderabad Karnataka Region has not been undertaken so far. Many aspects of Veerashaiva community are still unknown to the scholars. At the same time no systamatic information about the social life of Veerashaiva widows of different region of Karnataka is available. That is why, an attempt is being made in a systematic manner to assess the integration of widows in Veerashaiva community.

The problems of integration of widows involves a study of the socio-economic background, educational level, occupation, integration of widows within family, neighbourhood and community. Such a study warrants the use of exploratory approach and field work. In case of Veerashaiva community it is extremely difficult to make available secondary data on the details of the population and other conditions of life. It is very difficult to know the number of widows in this community. To overcome it, I have contacted religious priests, district treasury office and Mahila Mandals and well known persons with public image to collect the names of widows in different parts of Gulbarga city.

To acquaint myself with the problems of widows, many journals, books, reports, gazetteers, encyclopaedia, published and unpublished theses and all other available secondary sources were studied.

The field work is undertaken in different areas of Gulbarga city. With the help of religious priests, community elders and government records a list of Veerashaiva widows was prepared by collecting 250 widows from different blocks where Veerashaivas are concentrated. We have covered the old blocks and also extension areas. All 250 widows are taken as sample for a detailed indepth inquiry and an interview schedule was prepared and used as a tool for collecting information regarding the profile and problems of Veerashaiva widows. The interview schedule deals with the demographic characters and information on the family and the socio-economic background of the Veerashaiva widows. It also deals with the factors which help them to integrate within the family, neighbourhood and community. Questions pertaining to their attitude towards remarriage and awareness regarding certain legislations were also included.

Due to non-availability of the list of Veerashaiva widows, I have collected names of widows from district treasury office which is providing financial assistance to widows on the recommendation of state government. To get an adequate representation of Veerashaiva widows from various socio-economic backgrounds, the different religious institutions (*Mathas*) headed by religious priests were visited. This helped me in getting a better perspective of the problems faced by Veerashaiva widows. Visits to various Mahila Mandals, helped me to prepare a list of widows belonging to middle and lower economic strata of the community. Contact through friends and relatives, and well-known persons of that particular area also helped me to identify many Veerashaiva widows. I have collected the names of widows through various agencies. I was in a position to get the names of 250 widows. They constitute the universe of my research and investigation.

During field work a few widows appeared to be more knowledgeable and cooperative. About a dozen and a half widows have been interviewed several times in order to have an indepth understanding of the life of widows. They formed the purposive sample for our investigation. It is said that "purposive sampling devotes the method of selecting a number of groups of units in such a way that selected groups together yield as quickly as possible the same averages and proportions as the totality has with respect of those characteristics which are already a matter of statistical knowledge"[35]. Purposive sampling is also called judgement sampling when the researcher purposively or deliberately selects certain samples or units for investigation from the universe, it is known as the purposive sampling[36]. First hand information and an indepth knowledge about the problem were collected through purposive sample.

My introduction to the Veerashaiva widows of Gulbarga city is through the elderly persons and leaders of Mahila Mandals and Akkana Balagas of those particular areas. Initially, two months were spent in getting acquainted with the informants. This was followed by general enquiries pertaining to the customs and practices of Veerashaiva people. Being an outsider and new to research work I required sufficient time to get an insight into the specificities of their behaviour. First hand information about the problem was collected during my pre-Ph.D. period itself.

After preparing a very comprehensive interview schedule a pilot study on a representative sample of Veerashaiva widows was made. On the basis of the analysis of the pilot study and the suggestions made by the supervisor the interview schedule was modified and finalised. The field work of interviewing as well as filling up an interview schedule was initiated on 8th August, 1991, and was completed on 25th December, 1991 and was resumed in January, 1992 and continued upto the end of March, 1992.

Though formal completion of interviewing the respondents was over, the visits to the field were continued. A constant touch with the members constituting the purposive sample was kept alive until the drafting of the thesis was over.

Since it is a sensitive area of research, the initial difficulties in establishing the rapport with the respondents were experienced. However these difficulties were overcome through the help from a few elderly widows and women folk of the area. Throughout my field work I used to take help from the elderly women, who worked for me as informants.

Many of the respondents being depressed in life and being uneducated, it was very difficult for me to make them understand the purpose of my visit to their houses. In the beginning some of the respondents started weeping when I asked about their deceased husbands and were found hesitant to answer the questions. They took me as an investigator sent by the Government to check the property held by them. Really, establishing rapport was a major problem with many widows. Some of them were quite suspicious and afraid of me and would not even allow me to enter into their houses. As Goode and Hatt (1952) rightly mentioned that "some respondents will feel ill at ease, at first, because they are afraid that they will have to answer difficult questions". They do not wish to be embarrassed by being unable to answer queries about international relations, impending legislation, and so on. Usually, however, this type of anxiety can be easily allayed by reassuring the persons that "this is just a survey, you know. There aren't any right or wrong answers, and this isn't a quiz. We are simply trying to find out how people feel"[37]. The researcher has been able to convince the respondents about the usefulness of the study and established a better rapport with them.

In some other cases the respondents themselves were ready to answer the questions, because they thought the researcher would help them in securing pensions for them. There were a few, who were not at all ready for interview without the permission of their in-laws. The researcher convinced them that in a scientific study no name of the interviewed was being recorded. She said to them "we simply record your opinions". I convinced the respondents who were in government services by saying that every thing would be kept confidential and there was no harm to their jobs.

On one occasion a lady started quarrelling with me by saying "why did you take all that information of my house from my mother in my absence?" I reassured her that the details of her family would be used only to analyse the problems of widowhood and their adjustment to the mainstream of life, and convinced her that the secrecy of information would be maintained.

I had to experience a number of similar situations during my field work. But eventually the situation changed and I became more familiar to them and afterwards no trouble was experienced.

During my period of research I used to visit the respondents often, in order to get free and frank opinions about the problem. With this method, it was possible to gain some insight into such sensitive topic (area). I have maintained a diary and all the events of the day-to-day activities have been recorded during the night. A great deal of difficulty was faced while working on subjects like reactions towards widowhood, feelings of in-laws towards them, details about their husbands. In fact widows, especially those who are educated seem to have adopted an ambivalent attitude towards the phenomenon.

The main and the most frequently used tool in the field work was observation. It is one of the primary research instruments. As Webbs puts it, "Deliberate and sustained personal observation is an indispensable part of the study of any social institution, even if the social institution itself is invisible and intangible in its wholeness"[38]. Since the family, neighbourhood and community have been treated as units in this study, the integration of widows in these units has been undertaken and they have been brought under observation. P.V. Young (1966) has defined observation "as deliberate study through the eye, which may be used as one of the methods for scrutinising collective behaviour and complex of institutions as well as separate units composing of totallity"[39]. Hence the significance of observation in this study.

During the course of field work it was found out that along with observation the face to face interview method was most suitable as it provided scope to get an indepth insight into the problems of the integration of widows. Hence the structured interview method was adopted to elicit information. In this work, I have used structural-functional approach.

The present study was undertaken with the main purpose of stuying in detail the problems of widows along with the process of integration. Such a method does not warrant the sophisticated statistical tools of analysis. In this study the stress is on qualitative approach. However, the simple statistical tools have been prepared only to highlight the qualification of certain observations.

REFERENCES

1. Sapru, R.K.: *Women and Development;* Ashish Publishing House, New Delhi, 1989, pp. 231.
2. Altekar, (Dr) A.S.: *Position of Women in Hindu Civilization from Prehistoric Times to the Present Day,* 1973.
3. Sapru, R.K.: *Women and Development,* Ashish Publishing House New Delhi, 1989, pp. 232.
4. *Ibid.*
5. Lopamudra: *The Plight of Widows, Social Welfare,* Feb.-March 1983, pp. 13.
6. Indira Kulshreshtha: *Women's Studies in School Education. A New 'Noopur' Perspective,* 1989, pp. 20.

7. *Ibid.*, p. 21.

8. Krishnakumari, N.S.: *Status of Single Women in India,* Uppal Publishing House Delhi, 1987, p. 68.

9. Manna, Samita (DR) and Chakravorty, Panchali.: Aged Widows of Bengal, Article in *Man and Life,* Vol.17, No.1 & 2, Jan-June 1991, pp. 1-2.

10. Barrett, C.J. : *Women in Widowhood in Sions—The Journal of Women in Culture and Society;* 1976, p. 856.

11. Das, F.M., *Purdah: The Study of Indian Women,* New York, Vanguard Press Inc., 1932, pp. 34, 77.

12. Angell, R.C. Quoted in, L. David Sills (ed); *International Encyclopedia of the Social Sciences,* Vol. 11, New-York, The McMillan Co., and The Free Press, 1968, p. 380.

13. Ganguli, B.N.: *"Emotional Integration and economic and Social Disparities"* in report of seminar on National Integration, Delhi; University Grants Commission, 1958, pp. 51-57.

14. Dhadve, M.S.: *Sociology of Slum,* Archives Books, New Delhi, 1989, p. 145.

15. Francesca, M. Cancian: "Varieties of Functional Analysis" in David Sills (Ed), *International Encyclopedia of the Social Sciences,,* Vol.6, New York, McMillan Company, 1968, p. 29.

16. Alex, Inkeles: *What is Sociology?;* Englewood Cliffs, Prentice Hall, 1964, pp. 34-35.

17. Francis M. Abraham: *Modern Sociological Theory An Introduction,* New Delhi, Oxford University Press, 1982, pp. 91.

18. Gillin and Gillin: *Cultural Sociology,* New York, McMillan, 1948, p. 551.

19. *Ibid:* p. 551.

20. *Ibid:* p. 552.

21. Anthony Giddens and Jonathan H. Turner: *Social Theory Today,* Polity Press, p. 189.

22. Talcott Parsons: Toward a general theory of action, quoted by Dr. B. K. Roy Burman in his article on sociology of national integration. A rapid review of concept and

problems; 10th Sociological Conference, 1970, Dec. p. 108.

23. Parson, Talcott: *Double Reference of the Concept of Integration Social Systems;* American Publication Company Pvt., New York, (1976) p. 36.
24. Mair, L.P. Criteria of an Integrational Society in studies in Applied Authropology; quoted by Dr. B. K. Roy Burman: working paper on national integration; Tenth Sociological Conference, 1970. p. 72.
25. Bottomore, T.B.: *Sociology as Social Criticism,* S. Chanda and Company Ltd. New Delhi, 1979, p. 20.
26. Francesca, M.C. Quoted in, *International Ecncylopedia of Social Sciences,* Vol. VI, New York; The McMillan Co., and The Free Press, 1968, p. 29.
27. Srinivas, M.V. : "The Changing Position of Indian Women", *Man 12(2);* 1976; pp. 221-224.
28. Parwathamma, C.: *Sociological Essays: Veerashaivism;* Popular Prakashan, Bombay, 1972.
29. Ramanamma: *Graduate Employed Women in India in an Urban Setting,* Poona, Dastane Ramchandra & Co., pp. 14.
30. Sushila Mehta: 1982; *Revolution and the Status of women in India,* p. 32.
31. Ghosh, S.K. : *Indian Women Through the Ages;* Ashish Publishing House, New Delhi, 1989.
32. Ila Mukherjee: *Social Status of North Indian Women (1526-1707 A.D.),* Shivalal Agarwala and Company Educational Publication, Agra, pp. 114-135.
33. Radha Devi, D.: *"Work Participation of Widows in India, A Census Analysis"*, a paper presented at the National Seminar on Widowhood in India, organised Jointly by Janata Shikshana Samiti, Dharwad and Sri Dharmasthala Manjunatheswrar Trust, Ujire, 1987.
34. Nagesh, H.V., Nair, P.S. and Katti, A.P. : *Widowhood in India,* Janata Shikshana Samiti, Dharwad, 1988.
35. Hamsarj: *Theory and Practice in Social Research;* Srijeet Publications, Delhi, 1987, p. 235.

36. Bajpai, (Dr). S.R.: *Methods of Social Survey and Research*, 1972, p. 149.
37. William J. Goode and K. Hatt: *Methods in Social Research* McGraw Hill Book Company, 1952, p. 191.
38. Sharma, B.A.V.: *Research Methods in Social Sciences*, Sterling Publishers Pvt. Ltd., New Delhi, 1984, p. 128.
39. *Ibid.*, p. 129.

2

Universe of the Study

2.1 Historical, Social and Cultural Background of Gulbarga District and City

2.1.1 Introduction

Gulbarga city is the headquarters of the Gulbarga district and also of the division. It is a rapidly growing town and is situated on the Madras-Bombay broadgauge railway line. It has remained as the premier city and the headquarters of the district ever since its formation in 1873. Earlier Gulbarga was known as Kalburgi which means a 'stony land' or 'stone roofing' or a 'heap of stones' in Kannada. Another version is that Gulbarga was so named to connote a leaf with flower, since 'GUL' means 'Flower' and 'BURG' means a leaf in the Persian language. The term Gulbarga perhaps signifies a place of beauty like a flower with a leaf. It is also possible that the name Gulbarga is associated with the name of one of its earlier rulers, viz., Raja Gulchand. Even now quite a large number of people from rural areas often refer to it by the old name. The fort at Gulbarga which is said to have been originally built by Raja Gulchand was subsequently strengthened by Alauddin Bahamani.

The Gulbarga town assumed a great prominence during the early Bahamani period when the founder of this dynasty (kingdom) shifted his capital from Daulatabad to Gulbarga. It continued to be the capital of this dynasty till about 1424 A.D. Thereafter gradually it lost its importance. Now there are a few remnants in the form of ancient monuments which testify its glorious past. The fort contained 15 towers and 26 guns of which one was 8 meters long. Within the ramparts of the fort there is the imposing mosque, which spanning an area of 72 meters by 59 meters, resembles the great mosque of Cordova in Spain. This mosque is the only one of its kind in the entire country.

In the eastern outskirts of the town there are several tombs of Bahamani sultans. These are huge structures with high domes. The tomb of Khwaja Bande Nawaz is venerated by Muslims and also by Hindus of the region. The annual prayer session is an event of considerable religious and social importance. The tomb of Khwaja Bande Nawaz is one of the chief tourist attractions of Gulbarga.

The other prominent shrine of equal importance but mainly to the Hindus is the shrine of lord Sharanabasaveshwara. Sharanabasaveshwara was an eminent religious teacher and philosopher who preached religious and social qualities. This temple has been developed into a pilgrim centre. Under its auspices an annual fair lasting for a fortnight is held during the month of April. Apart from these two shrines, there are two groups of royal tombs which are also of some tourist interest. One of these is located close to the southern entrance of the fort, and the other is located in the eastern outskirts.

Though not a major industrial city, Gulbarga has a number of factories of which the M.S.K. Mill is the biggest. There are several smaller industrial establishments such as dhal factory, saw mill, iron workshop, oil mill and beedi factory.

Gulbarga has stolen a march over many other district headquarters in the state in point of educational progress. There are several colleges and higher secondary schools and high schools for boys and girls. One of the attractions of the town is the public garden, Mahboob Gulshan maintained by the municipal corporation, which is situated by the road leading from the railway station to the main bazaar.

2.1.2 *Geographical Location of Gulbarga District*

Gulbarga district is located in the north-eastern sector of Karnataka and covers a vast expanse of table-land that lies between the latitudinal parallels 76°03′ E and 77°42′ E, and latitudinal parallels of 16°12′ N and 17°46′ N. On the north-west, for a short stretch, the district shares its borders with Solapur and Osmanabad districts of Maharastra and on the east it is bounded by the districts of Medak and Mahaboobnagar of Andra Pradesh. On the other three sides, Gulbarga district is sourrounded by territories belonging to Karnataka state itself; Bidar district in the north, Raichur district on the south and Bijapur district on the west. The river Krishna runs in the southern side of Gulbarga district and forms the natural boundary between Gulbarga and Raichur districts. On the western sector, for a short distance the Bhima divides the lands belonging to the districts of Gulbarga and Bijapur and forms the natural boundary between the two districts (1981 census)[1].

2.1.3 *Climate*

The district is situated in the region which is generally known as the Deccan Plateau. As per the physio-agronomic classification of the areas within the state, Gulbarga belongs to the northern maidan region. The total area of the district is 16,224 square kilometres. Its population "according to the 1991 census was 25,82,169. Its rural population was 19,72,366 urban population 6,09,803. This district has its male population 13,15,848 and female population 12,66,321.

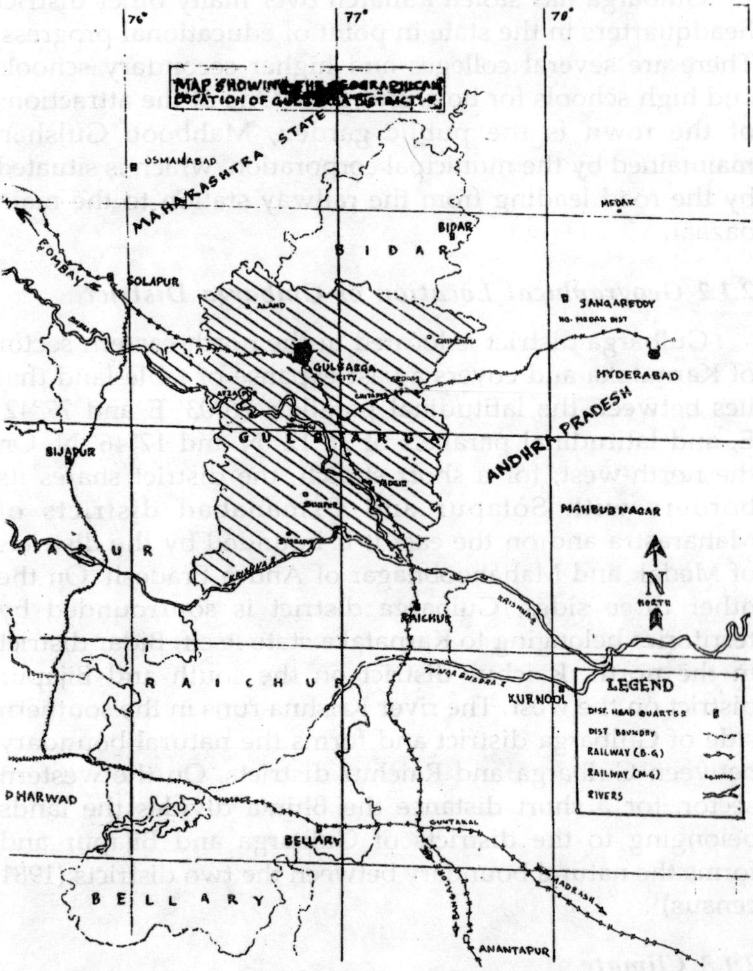

Gulbarga district enjoys a dry but healthy climate. Though the summer heat is somewhat excessive as compared to several other districts of the state, it cannot be categorised as extremely hot. The temperature begins to rise steadily with the commencement of the summer season from about the middle of February. Simultaneously humidity decreases day by day. This season lasts till about the first week of June. Usually, May happens to be the hottest month of the year and on several days the maximum temperature would shoot up to 45° celsius. The rainy season sets in during June and lasts till the end of September. Thereafter the months of November and December mark the period of the post monsoons.

The period from December to mid-February is regarded as the winter season and the intensity of cold increases towards the end of December, which happens to be the coldest month of the year. The district lies in a region in which the rainfall is moderate to low besides being quite capricious. The average annual rainfall is 715 mm., and there would on an average be 47 raindays spread over six-month period. Usually September is the month with a heavy rainfall.

2.1.4 History of Gulbarga District

During the early Christian era Gulbarga district was under the supreme power of Satavahanas. For about three centuries it was surrounded by the Vakatakas. Even some parts of Bellary district were influenced by them, and extended their influence towards a wider area. The south Indian history is famous for the period of Rastrakutas' ascendancy in the Deccan and Gulbarga district is proud of its association with this dynasty. They made 'Malkhed' as capital of Gulbarga district. Rastrakutas' rule ended in 973 A.D. due to the independence declared by the feudatories of Chalukya dynasty. For about 200 years Gulbarga district remained under the control of Chalukya rulers who made Basavakalyan of Bidar district as their capital.

In early times, Gulbarga was a Hindu city of great extent. Prior to the Mohammedan conquest, Gulbarga was included in the dominions of the Rajas of Warangal. "It is stated that after the subjugation of the Yadavas of Deogiri (Daulatabad) by the Mohammadens other inroads were made by the subsequent invaders, which resulted in the overthrow of the Hindu Kingdom of Warangal. In the year 1323 AD Alagh Khan (afterwards the emperor Md. Tughlak) was deputed by his father Ghazi Baig Tughlak to suppress a rebellion that had broken out in the southern portions of the Kingdom. He also captured Gulbarga and Bidar. Twenty years later the Deccan Governors rebelled against the emperor Mohammad Tughlak and setup a Kingdom of their own. Malik Magh, the nominee of the rebels abdicated in favour of Jafar Khan, who assumed the title of Alauddin Hasan Shah Gangu Bahmani. He selected Gulbarga as his capital in 1347 AD and began to rule the new region. The new king rapidly extended his dominions which were subsequently divided into 4 great provinces. In 1432 AD, the capital was transferred to Bidar. Towards the close of the 15th century Gulbarga came into the possession of the kings of Bijapur.[2]" Thereafter Gulbarga lost its importance and gradually reverted to its earlier status of a provincial town. On the conquest of the Deccan by Aurangzeb, it was again included in the empire of Delhi but after the establishment of the British suzerainty, Gulbarga district remained as a part of the Nizam's dominions.

After the reorganization of states on November 1, 1956 Gulbarga became a part of Mysore state, which is now known as Karnataka. Hence, Gulbarga city as a part of Karnataka state has rich cultural and traditional heritage. Gulbarga occupied a unique place in the history of Karnataka and southern part of India, with the legacy of art, architecture, literature, commerce and religious practices. Today, Gulbarga is unique place of meeting different religious, linguistic and regional groups. All groups have contributed their mite towards the development of a composite culture.

2.1.5 Universe of the Study

Though the Veerashaivas are spread over the entire length and breadth of the state, there are certain districts, which have larger concentration of Veerashaiva population than others. In this study I have restricted myself to the Veerashaiva widows of Gulbarga city. Though there are different areas/wards/blocks in Gulbarga city where

Veerashaiva population is scattered, for my investigation I have selected the wards/areas/blocks where the Veerashaiva population is concentrated. Care is taken to choose the respondents not only from traditional city areas, but also from extension areas. Jagat, Shahabazar, Maqudumpur, Brahampur belong to the traditional category, while Godutai Nagar, Khuba plot, Santinagar, Santosh Colony are included in the second category.

According to the census report of 1991, the population of Gulbarga city is 3,03,139. And it has been divided into 11 municipal wards/blocks. They are mentioned as below.

Table 2.1: Blockwise/ Wardwise Population of Gulbarga City

Sl.No.	*Wards*	*No. of occupied residential houses*	*No. of houses*	*Population*		
				Male	*Female*	*Total*
1	Station bazar	7235	7622	22654	20472	43126
2	Jagat	3377	3974	12889	10778	23667
3	Gazipur	5059	5844	18726	16127	34853
4	Maqudumpur	3886	3951	12964	11744	24708
5	Rauza	4245	4850	16676	15244	31920
6	Mominpura A	1910	1915	7183	6690	13873
7	Mominpura B	4174	4509	16226	14686	30912
8	Asif Gunj	3855	4406	13410	12493	25903
9	Shahbazar	4266	4604	13947	12746	26693
10	Brahmpur A	2553	2693	7806	6911	14717
11	Brahmpur B	6000	6000	16838	15929	32767
Total		48560	50368	159319	143820	03139

Source: 1991 Census of Gulbarga District.

The universe of my research is Jagat, Maqdumpura, Shahabazar, Brahampur, which comes under the block numbers 2, 4, 9, 10, respectively and Godutai Nagar, Khubha Plot, Santi Nagar and Santosh Colony under block number 1.

2.2 The Reasons for Choice of Universe

There are several works on widows and rehabilitation of widows. But there are a few works on the widows living in specific communities. Although the status of widows by and large may appear to be the same, there are bound to be differentiation of statuses on account of different social and cultural contexts in which they make their living. The specific religions and cultural rigidities in a

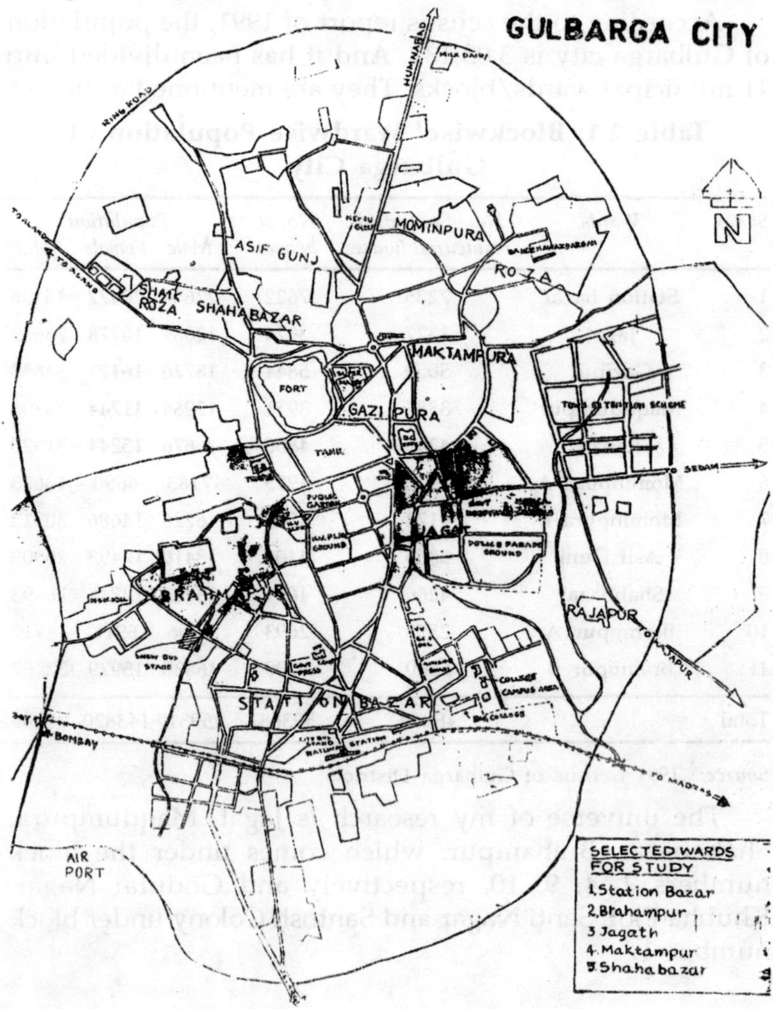

community influence the course of living of its members. In some communities they may be liberal and/or very rigid. That is why it would not be appropriate if we consider the status of widows in Hindu and Muslim communities as similar. The same logic holds true when we discuss the problems of widows belonging to different communities. One of the main reasons for choosing this theme is to understand the problems of widows at depth. Gulbarga city has been selected in order to study the integration of widows in Veerashaiva community.

Gulbarga has been the centre of activities of Veerashaivas, for a very long time Veerashaivas have been in agriculture, business and services. They have established Veerashaiva Vidya Vardhak Sangha in the year 1918 to propagate the ideas of Veerashaivism. It has made successful attempts to spread education through establishing a network of educational institutions. Today there are several educational institutions managed by this sangha. Besides, there are several religious institutions which have been active in spreading the message of Veerashaivism.

Veerashaivas occupy an important place in the composition of Gulbarga population. Education, agriculture and business have revolutionised their way of living. This community is exposed to all forces of modernisation. Again their separate identity provided in 1991 census indicates that they constitute a community with its specific beliefs and practices. It is this, that made me to treat Veerashaivas different from other communities. Earlier, they formed a part of Hindu community. But now it is not so. The belief patterns sharply differ and hence the differentiation in their system of living.

Another reason for the choice of Veerashaiva community is to assess the status of widows in the context of liberal religious values, emphasizing equality and unity. Since Gulbarga fulfils most of the conditions contemplated by the researcher, the city of Gulbarga has been selected for the purpose of investigation. The areas where the

Veerashaiva population is concentrated have been identified and selected. While selecting them care is taken to bring into focus the traditional areas situated in the city and modernised areas situated at the outskirts of the city.

I have selected Brahmpur, Shahbazar areas which are spread in the areas where the holy temple of Sharana Basaveshwar is located. The Veerashaivas living around the temple daily offer their prayers and perform religious activities arranged on behalf of temple authorities.

2.3 A Profile of Veerashaivas of Gulbarga

Gulbarga is inhabited by a number of religious groups. Among them Veerashaivas occupy an important place owing to their number, possession of resources and participation in city life. They are living in different localities of the city. Right from the beginning we do not have any source with the help of which their population could be recorded. Another difficulty is that they have been included in the category of Hindus. A rough estimate may make us believe that Veerashaivas constitute about 25% of the population of Gulbarga city.

It is said that from time immemorial Veerashaiva religion has survived in India with other religions. It is acclaimed as a very progressive religion since it stresses on equality. About the population of Veerashaivas of Bombay state, the Mysore state and Madras state, Sadasivaiah (1967) has mentioned, "the total number of Lingayats in Bombay state is 13,70,023 according to 1931 census, 83,557 in Mysore state according to 1911 census, and 1,70,013 in Madras state according to 1921 census"[4].

The Veerashaivas are also called by another name as Lingayats. Estimating the Veerashaiva population, Srinivas M.N. says, "In the united Karnataka, it has been estimated that a little more than 20% of the population may be Lingayats"[5]. Ishwaran has stated around 20% of total population of Karnataka, every fifth person of the state population is a Lingayat. Indeed, every second person in the three most important districts of northern Karnataka viz., Bijapur, Belgaum and Dharwar is a Lingayat[6]. In Gulbarga the percentage seems to be a bit high.

In recent past several Veerashaiva organisations have struggled to convince the census authorities to provide a separate column for Lingayats in their proforma. They intend to have a separate identity and do not want to be merged in Hindu community. Their efforts to provide a higher status to Veerashaiva community are still to yield the desired results.

Veerashaivism was existing since centuries, but it was unknown and was not popularised. In the 12th century it was elevated to its glorious heights of sublimity revitalised by Basava and other Sharanas. The establishment of 'Anubhava Mantapa' or the Religious Parliament made Veerashaivism to reach the peak of celestial heights. The Shivasharanas opened the gates of religion to one and all with a sense of equality. At the hands of Basava and others Veerashaiva religion grew and enriched itself and it attained its transcendental height. In a short span of time many sharanas from every nook and corner came together with their divine and mystic experiences and developed the Veerashaiva religion, and it also attracted the people of different castes, creeds, sects and communities.

It is through Veerashaiva religion that Kayak-Dasoha principles were exposed to the light by Sharanas. Even Veerashaivas of Gulbarga also practised these principles from many decades. It was more popular at the time of Shri Sharanabasaveshwar. From 18th century the Veerashaivas of neighbouring villages started Kayaka-Dasoha. With a view to popularising Veerashaivism and spreading its message, many Mathas were built in Gulbarga. Therefore we have a rich cultural heritage which was built and patronised by these Mathadhishas, Shivasharanas, Saints and Seers. Moreover, the Veerashaivas of Gulbarga have contributed considerably to the development of Gulbarga and the region.

2.3.1 Contribution of Veerashaivas to the Social Life of Gulbarga

In Gulbarga Veerashaiva community is known for several reasons. An important and a single contribution to the present day Veerashaiva community is in the field of education. Hundreds of educational institutions have been founded and are being run by the Mathas and other Veerashaiva organisations.

The contribution of Swamijis, Mathas and other religious organisations to the field of religion and literature is also considerable. Some of them are much interested in publishing the books and spreading the knowledge about Veerashaiva religion, culture and philosophy. The cultural and philosophical activities of Veerashaivas of Gulbarga are as important as other educational activities. In the following pages an attempt is being made to highlight the contributions of Veerashaivas.

The contributions of Veerashaivas of Gulbarga in the field of education are very significant as they gave a new turn of events to the general living of the people. The number of educational institutions run by Veerashaiva Mathadishas and other institutions in Gulbarga have achieved substantially in the field of art, culture, science and technology. The spirit behind their great achievement is the great culture of Kayaka-Dasoha endowed by their forefathers. The Dasoha culture was practised personally and socially by their forefathers. The religious beliefs have been institutionalised and universalised through establishing educational institutions. One such institution is run by Shri Sharanabasaveshwar Vidya Vardhak Sangha, which was established in the year 1918 by Mahadasohi Poojya Doddappa Appa. It is one of the important Veerashaiva institutions in Gulbarga, which has its branch in Basavakalyan. Today it has around twenty educational institutions which are serving the people of Gulbarga. Apart from it, even there are number of Mathas in Gulbarga like, Chauda-puri Hiremath Brahampur, Shri

Revanasiddeshwar Gadduge Math Maktampur, Guru Basaveshwar Brahan Math Maktanpur, Kenchbasava Swami Matha Roza, Kallimath Gazipura, Hiremath Shahabazar, Sulpul Math Shahabazar, ParsiMath Shahabazar, Shadakshari Math Maktampur, Mallikarjun Math Ashif Gunj and Chan-dankeri Math Jagat, which are headed by the Mathadhishas. Some of these Mathadhishas have established a number of educational institutions and have provided the boarding facilities to the students. One such educational institution is Shri Gurubasaveshwar Shikshana Samsthe (1982).

Some other Mathas are undertaking only the religious activities by organising bhajanas, puranas, pravachanas and other religious discourses for the spread of Veerashaivism. There are some other Mathas which are undertaking both educational as well as religious activities. Apart from these there are in the city other associations run by Veerashaivas which are established to promote the cause of education. They are Shanteshwar Education Society, Mahantappa Allad Education Society, Akkamahadevi Education Society, Basaveshwar Primary School etc.

The Veerashaivas of Gulbarga have contributed their mite for the growth of trade, commerce and agriculture. The educational institutions established by them have helped not only the Veerashaiva community but also the people belonging to other communities. Consequent to this, we find among Veerashaivas a large number of doctors, engineers lawyers, administrators, ministers, chief ministers and national leaders. Thus the Veerashaivas of Gulbarga also have their share in promoting science, engineering and medicine in this region. They are practising diverse professions, ranging from agriculture and industry to holding of important political portfolios.

Politics is another important aspect of Veerashaivas of Gulbarga. A number of prominent persons have the unique honour of participating in the freedom struggle. Many of them have gone underground and fought with the divisive forces. After attainment of freedom a large number of Veerashaivas have joined the political mainstream and occupied important positions in the party and the Government. The Veerashaiva community attained the status of a dominant caste. Thus, we notice the full-fledged participation of Veerashaivas in almost all walks of life.

The role of Veerashaiva literature is very commendable and conspicuous in enriching the Kannada literature. Gulbarga has been a home of many literary persons, poets, novelists, prose writers, vachana writers and others who have been continuously contributing to the growth of Kannada literature. Many literary persons like Dr. P.S. Shankar, Dr. M.S. Lathe, Dr. M.G. Biradar, Dr. S.M. Hiremath, Dr. Basavaraj Sabarad got awards and were honoured for their contributions to the field of Kannada literature. Even many Veerashaiva women of Gulbarga are *vachanakartis*. It is an impressive and promising trend that the Veerashaivas of Gulbarga are gaining good places in writing of poetry, drama, fiction, short story, criticism etc. They are working even in the field of research.

The Veerashaivas of Gulbarga have made unique contribution in the field of music. Sharanabasaveshwar institution is providing education in music upto graduation level. This institution has also prepared many cassettes of 'Bhakti' sangeeta extracting the songs from Basava and other vachanakaras. These songs were sung by many great musicians. Among them Jambaladinni got award for his melodious music. Hence the Veerashaivas of Gulbarga have given equal importance to music. They earned name and fame not only in the region but also at the national level.

The Veerashaivas of Gulbarga are rich even in the field of painting. Throughout Karnataka Gulbarga district has laid more stress on modern art and art education. The city of Gulbarga has got great artists that have earned both the state and national level fame. One of the Veerashaiva institutions runs postgraduation course in painting and many have started the research work in this field. Gulbarga has great artists like G.S. Khanderao, V.G. Aandani, Shantalingappa Patil, M.T. Bhopati, S.M. Pandit, Shankarao Alandakar, Vijaya Hagargundagi, Kumar Chandrashekar, etc., Sri Khanderao and V.G. Aandani have started Ideal Fine Art society in the year 1965 and Kalaniketan respectively. They have been known to the people through arranging exhibitions of their individual art creations.

Veerashaivas of Gulbarga have contributed for the spread of Veerashaiva philosophy. Veerashaivas believe that Istalinga is symbol of knowledge and Vibhuti and Rudrakshi are the light and eyes of Shiva for having a religious sanctity. They wear Istalinga on their body. They do not worship Sthavaralinga which is installed in the form of idol. This principle is also followed by many of the Veerashaivas of Gulbarga. They perform many special religious activities in Shravana Masa. All Veerashaiva Mathas and religious institutions conduct special lectures and puranas for depicting the life and teachings of Veerashaiva saints (Shivasharanaru) in which Veerashaivas take active part. They give donations to many religious institutions and Mathas which are providing free boarding and educational facilities to the poor Veerashaiva students. Mahadasoha Peethadhipati of Sharanabasaveshwara Samsthan, the Mathadhipatis of various Mathas are the guiding force for the Veerashaivas of Gulbarga city and its surrounding areas.

The Veerashaiva women of Gulbarga have been contributing their mite for the propagation of Veerashaiva ideas by playing different roles at home and outside home. Apart from fulfilling the obligations of a mother, wife and daughter, they have organised themselves into small associations known as Akkana Balaga and Mahila Mandal. Due to modernisation they have an access to education, services and other occupations. Some of the important women's organisations functioning in the city are Vasavi Mahila Mandal, Sangameshwar Mahila Mandal, Godutai

Mahila Mandal, Akkamahadevi Akkanabalaga etc. The members of Mahila Mandals are conducting cultural activities and encouraging the artistic talents. They have also undertaken the task of creating awareness about family planning among women folk. They have arranged classes to train women for various jobs such as craft, embroidery, tailoring etc. Several educated women have joined services in educational institutions, banks and offices. They are exposed to outside environment. Thus Veerashaiva women like other women have their contribution to the public life in Gulbarga. Women poets, novelists, researchers and politicians are significant as they contribute toward the progress of the city and the region.

The contributions of the Veerashaivas of Gulbarga have attracted the attention of many Veerashaiva people of neighbouring villages and they have migrated to this city and have been benefited in many fields. Thus the Veerashivas of Gulbarga have contributed to the culture of the region from many points of view.The concept of Istalinga, a symbol of one's own self, the idea of *shatsthala*; six fold evolution of the self-realization through monotheistic devotion with the grace of Guru-Linga-Jangama, Kayaka, a compulsory social duty by one and all in all walks of life. Dasoha Shivayoga, not in the traditional sense of yoga, but in the new form of day-today living, and acceptance of the Mundane life as real and worth living, are the unique contributions of Veerashivas of Gulbarga.

2.4 Demographic Characteristics of Respondents

An analysis of the demographic background of the respondents has its special significance. This may help us to understand how different variables such as age, educational level, occupation level etc., affect attitudes and behaviour patterns. Mannheim (1936) rightly said "the opinions, statements, proportions and systems of ideas are not taken at their face value but are interpreted in the light of the life situation of the one who expressed them". Thus the sociologists are interested in the study of the social background of their subjects.

This part of thesis specifically focuses upon the demographic characteristics of Veerashaiva widows under investigation. This will enable us to understand the different levels of living with their attributes. The findings pertaining to their personal characteristics and family back-ground, their educational level, age at the time of marriage and at the time of their husband's death, their occupational status, income, their subcaste composition, etc., have been covered in the study. This part not only provides a profile of Veerashaiva widows, but also gives an insight into the factors that may be found relevant in the analysis of their integration.

2.4.1 Age Composition of the Respondents

It is necessary to understand the age of respondents, because the effect of loss of spouse varies from age to age. The table given below depicts the age composition of the respondents.

Table 2.2: Distribution of Respondents by age

SI. No.	*Age Group*	*Frequency*	*Percentage*
1	10-20	2	0.8
2	21 - 30	17	6.8
3	31 -40	38	15.2
4	41 - 50	58	23.2
5	51 - 60	68	27.2
6	61 - 70	45	18.0
7	> 70	22	8.8
Total	-	250	100.0

The above table shows the percentage distribution of the Veerashaiva widows of Gulbarga city by age-group. 0.8% of our respondents are in the age group of 10-20 years, 6.8% in the age group of 21-30, 15.2% in the age group of 31-40, 23.2% in the age group of 41-50, 27.2% in the age group of 51-60, 18.0% in the age group of 61-70 and 8.8% in the age group of 71 and above. From the table above it is observed that, most of the respondents are in the age group of 51-60. The percentage of widows increases as we move from one age group to another upto the age group of 51-60 and afterwards it declines in the percentage of widows by their increasing age.

2.4.2 *Sub-Caste Composition of the Respondents*

It is necessary to know the sub-caste composition of respondents, because Veerashaiva community consists of different occupations. Sometimes sub-caste and occupation seem to be correlated. Even the problems of widows vary from one subcaste to other. The following table describes the subcaste composition of the respondents.

Table 2.3

Distribution of the Respondents by Subcaste

Sl. No.	*Sub-caste*	*Frequency*	*Percentage*
1	Jangamas	36	14.4
2	Panchamas	40	16.0
3	Dikshas	90	36.0
4	Adi Banajigas	47	18.8
5	Nekars or Jadaru	17	6.8
6	Akkasaligas or Shilvant	4	1.6
7	Ganigas	2	0.8
8	Kudavakkaligas	1	0.4
9	Gavaligas	4	1.6
10	Shiva Simpigas	2	0.8
11	Reddis	2	0.8
12	Hugars	1	0.4
13	Kumbar (Lingayat)	4	1.6
Total		250	100.0

The above table indicates the percentage distribution of Veerashaiva widows by sub-caste. It is noticed that there are 13 sub-castes among the respondents. Out of the total 250 widows 14.4% (36) are Jangamas, 16.0% (40) are Panchamas, 36.0% (90) are Dikshas, 18.8% (47) are Adi Banajigas, 6.8% (17) are Nekars or Jadaru, 1.6% (4) are Shilavants, 0.8% (2) are Ganigas, 0.4% (1) are Kudavakkaligas, 1.6% (4) are Gavaligas, 0.8% (2) are Reddis, 0.4%(1) are Hugars and 1.6%(4) are Kumbars (Lingayat).

From the above table it is inferred that the highest percentage of widows come from Diksha sub-caste while the lowest percentage from Kudavakkligas and Hugars. This is on account of the highest percentage of Diksha Veerasaivas constituting the total population of the community. There are numerous subcastes among Veerashaivas on the basis of various types of occupations performed by them. Nearly 85% of these subcastes have agriculture as a predominant occupation consisting of Jangamas, Panchamas, Dikshas and Adi Banajigas. While 14.8% have various occupations consisting of Ganigas, Kudavakkaligas, Gavaligas, Hugars, Kumbars, Simpigas, Akkasaligas, etc.

2.4.3 Educational Composition of the Respondents

Understanding of educational composition of the respondents is necessary in order to find out the level of education as it determines the acquisitions of knowledge, skill and abilities. The level of living is also indicated by this factor. The table given below explains the educational composition of the respondents.

Table 2.4: Educational Composition of the Respondents

Sl. No.	*Level of Education*	*Frequency*	*Percentage*
1	Illiterate	171	68,1
2	Primary	30	12.0
3	Middle	25	10.0

4	High School	15	6.0
5	College - no degree	4	1.6
6	Graduate	3	1.2
7	Post-Graduate	2	0.8
Total		250	100.0

The above table depicts the educational status of the widows. The widows have been classified into seven groups of which 68.4% widows are illiterate, 12.0% are able to read and write, 10.0% are educated upto middle school level, 6.0% are educated upto secondary level, 1.6% widows belong to Pre-University level, 1.2% widows are educated upto graduation level and only 0.8%(2) widows are educated upto postgraduate level.

The figures reveal that adequate importance is not given to provide education to women among Veerashaivas. In the absence of education it becomes necessary for them to depend on the other members of the family for their living. Nearly 90% of them appear to have almost nominal to nil education.

2.4.4 Economic Conditions

The economic conditions of the respondents were analysed in terms of their level of income. For this purpose 4 categories of income level have been constructed, viz.: *1)* No income, *2)* Low income, *3)* Middle income, *4)* High income. No income group of widows are those who do not have any independent source and are living in the family by contributing their labour in household activities. Low income group is characterised upto Rs. 10,000 and those who have their income between Rs. 10,001 and 30,000 are included in the middle income group. The respondents whose income is Rs. 30,001 and above are included in high income group. The table given below describes the economic conditions of respondents.

Table 2.5
Distribution of Respondents by their Income

SI. No.	*Income group*	*Frequency*	*Percentage*
1	No income	121	48.4
2	Low income	104	41.6
3	Middle income	19	7.6
4	High income	6	2.4
Total		250	100.0

The above table shows the percentage distribution of economic condition of widows by their income group. From the table it is observed that 121 constituting 48.4% widows belong to the no income group. Since most of the respondents belonged to joint family environment, they did not feel the necessity to go in for a job immediately. The widows in such families have contributed their mite in the form of household work. Their work is not composed as economic activity. 104 (41.6%) widows belong to low income group, 19 (7.6%) widows belong to middle income group while 6 (2.4%) widows belong to high income group, who are engaged in one or the other job.

It can be seen from the table that the highest percentage of widow's economic position is very low due to the death of the major earner of the family. While the lowest percentage of widow's economic position is good on account of their better economic condition of the family.

2.4.5 *Occupational Composition*

An attempt is made to analyse the occupational composition of the respondents. While a large number of them do not have any occupation which is remunerative. a few of them have been gainfully employed in different occupations. The table given below indicates the occupational composition of the widows under study.

Table 2.6: Occupational Status of the Respondents

Sl. No.	Occupation	Frequency	Percentage
1	Householder	168	67.2
2	Teacher	5	2.0
3	Lecturer	1	0.4
4	Doctor	1	0.4
5	Aya	5	2.0
6	S.D.C.	2	0.8
7	Peon	10	4.0
8	Coolie or Servant	46	18.4
9	Managing the field	2	0.8
10	Tailor	4	1.6
11	Vegetable seller	2	0.8
12	Dairy farming	1	0.4
13	Shop keeper	1	0.4
14	Coconut seller	2	0.8
Total		250	100.0

The above table depicts the occupational status of the respondents. It shows that 168 (67.2%) respondents are householders, who are leading a dependent life, 5 (2.0%) respondents are teachers, a single (0.4%) is a lecturer who started doing this job after her husband's death in order to free her from mental worries and to become economically independent, 1 (0.4%) respondent is a doctor, who is enjoying better economic position even before widowhood as well as after widowhood, 5 (2.0%) respondents are Ayas who joined this job after the death of their husbands to make their living, 2 (0.8%) respondents were appointed as S.D.C. in the places of their husbands, 10 (4.0%) respondents are peons, 46 (18.4%) respondents are coolies, 2 (0.8%) respondents are managing the field in order to protect their husbands' property, 4 (1.6%) respondents are tailors who are doing this job even before the death of their husbands to support the family income and provide stability to the economic conditions of family, 2 (0.8%) are engaged in selling the vegetables, a single (0.4%) respondent is engaged in dairy farming, 1 (0.4%) respondent is doing business on a small-scale, and 2 (0.8%) respondents are coconut sellers. It can be inferred from the table given above that a large number of widows have been living as dependants in the families of their husbands and only a few of them have made new ventures to be independent from their husband's families. They appear to have become integrated with the families of their husbands.

2.4.6 Age Composition of the Respondents at the Time of their Marriage

Marriage is regarded as a significant institution through which an individual makes an attempt to realise the cultural goals. It is an important affair in one's life since it entails new responsibilities on the married both socially and economically. In every religion, especially among Hindus marriage is a sacrament, and after marriage the couple have to abide by certain religious injunctions. So in order to bear the responsibilities of the married life, the bride and the bride-groom should attain the age of perfect maturity and understanding. So it is the common practice of the advanced sections of society or of the advanced households to postpone marriages to the proper ages. Sharada Act of (1929) lays down that a girl should be at least 14 years, and a boy of 18 years at the time of her or his marriage respectively. Early marriages are considered as offence and liable to punishment. Hence, now-a-days early marriages and child marriages are not in vogue. But yet they have not been totally prohibited. The table given below shows the age of each of the 250 respondents at the time of their marriages.

Table 2.7: Distribution of Respondents by Age at the Time of Their Marriage

Sl. No.	Age group	Frequency	Percentage
1	Upto 5 years	19	7.6
2	6-10 years	35	14.0
3	11-15 years	133	53.2
4	16-20 years	49	19.6
5	21 - 25 years	12	4.8
6	26 - 30 years	1	0.4
7	31 years and above	1	0.4
Total		250	100.0

In the above table there are 19 (7.6%) cases of marriages of brides below 10 years, and 35 (14.0%) cases in the range of 6-10 years of age, 133 (53.2%) respondents got married when they were in the age group of 11-15 years, 49 (19.6%) respondents got married when they were in the age group of 16-20 years, 12 (4.8%) respondents got married when they were in the age group of 21-25 years, 1 (0.4%) respondent got married in the age group of 26-30 years and a single respondent got married in the age group of 31 years and above. As stated by the respondents, the age group of 16-20 years is better for marrying of girls. It can be inferred that nearly 75% of the respondents age at the time of marriage was below 15 years. This showed the continuance of child marriage a few decades ago among Veerashaivas. The data revealed that only about 25% respondents have married at the age of 16 years and above.

2.4.7 Age Composition of Widows at the Time of their Widowhood

The crisis of widowhood and the age of respondents at the time of their husband's death are interrelated. The table given below reveals the age composition of respondents by their widowhood.

Table 2.8: Distribution of Respondents by Their Age at the Time of Their Husband's Death

SI. No.	*Age group*	*Frequency*	*Percentage*
1	10 - 20	17	6.8
2	21 - 30	65	26.0
3	31 - 40	62	24.8
4	41 - 50	50	20.0
5	51 - 60	41	16.4
6	61 - 70	15	6.0
8	> 70	00	0.0
Total		250	100.0

The statistical data represent the percentage distribution of widows by age at widowhood. The highest percentage (26.0) of widows lost their husbands at the age group of 21 to 30 years. The lowest percentage (6.0) of widows lost their husbands at the age of 61 to 70 years. 17 (6.8%) respondents became widowed at the age of 10 to 20 years, 62 (24.8%) respondents became widowed at the age of 31 to 40 years, 50 (20.0%) became widowed at the age of 41 to 50 years, while 41 (16.4%) became widowed at the age of 51 to 60 years. It further reveals that most of (62) the respondents became widowed in their middle age itself due to their early marriage. Thus the number of widows in their old age are very few (15) constituting the 6.0% of total respondents. It is also inferred from the data that nearly 32.0% of the respondents who would have gone in for remarriage remained widow's despite the permission to do so. It seems the demands of social Ethos prevalent have prevented them and preferred to spend their lite as widows rather than remarried house wives. This indicates the adherence to the accepted norms of life whether they form the core of faith they practice or not.

2.4.8 Duration of Widowhood

The effect of widowhood varies from one respondent to another, because of their variation in duration of widowhood. This duration of widowhood will help us to understand their problems more vividly and the period of their stress and strain. It has a direct relationship to the process of integration. It is during the early period of widowhood, there appears to be a problem of integration of widows in family, neighbourhood and community. The table given below illustrates the situation.

Table 2.9: Distribution of Respondents by Their Duration of Widowhood

Sl. No.	*Duration*	*Frequency*	*Percentage*
1	upto 2 years	33	13.2
2	3 - 5	37	14.8
3	6- 8	30	12.0
4	9 - 11	40	16.0
5	12 - 14	22	8.8
6	15 - 17	13	5.2
7	18 - 20	26	10.4
8	21 - 23	5	2.0
9	24 - 26	7	2.8
10	27 - 29	3	1.2
11	30 and above	34	13.6
Total		250	100.0

The statistical data provide a clear picture of the duration of widowhood of the respondent. It shows that 13.2% of the respondents are leading a life of widowhood, from 2 years, 14.8% respondents are widowed from 3-5 years, 12.0% are widowed from 6-8 years, 16.0% are widowed from 9-11 years, 8.8% are widowed from 12-14 years, 5.2% are widowed from 15-17 years, 10.4% are widowed from 18-20 years, 2.0% are widowed from 21-23 years, 2.8% are widowed from 24-26 years, 1.2%) are widowed from 27-29 years, 13.6% are widowed from 30 and plus years. It can be observed from above table that majority of the respondents are leading a life of widowhood from 10 years. Duration of widowhood varied from just 3 months to 40 years. The length of widowhood speaks of the duration of sufferings of the widows.

2.4.9 Settlement of Respondents in Gulbarga

It is necessary to know the settlement of respondents in Gulbarga, to analyse the way of living, way of thinking to that of migrated widows after their widowhood. The below table depicts the settlement of respondents in Gulbarga.

Table 2.10: Distribution of Respondents by Their Settlement in Gulbarga

SI. No.	*Response (period)*	*Frequency*	*Percentage*
1	1 - 5 years	63	25.2
2	6-10 years	80	32.0
3	11 and above (Native of Gulbarga)	107	42.8
Total		250	100.0

After the death of husbands, women face a breakdown and crisis in their economic conditions. To earn something for their livelihood they moved towards Gulbarga city from their native places. The above table shows the respondent's settlement in Gulbarga city. About 25.2% of respondents have settled in Gulbarga since five years. 32.2% of widows have settled in this city for searching occupation or job after widowhood. While 42.8% of widows have settled in Gulbarga from 11 and above years.

From the above table it is inferred that the highest

percentage (42.8%) of widows settled in Gulbarga from the beginning. They did not face problems of adjustment like other widows who moved to city after becoming widows. While the medium percentage of (32.0%) widows settled in this place in order to get themselves engaged in one or the other income generating activity for their livelihood, where as the lowest number of (25.2%) widows settled in Gulbarga before their husband's death on account of educating their children and their husband's employment in this particular city. This helped them to settle even after their widowhood.

This background of the Veerashaiva widows of Gulbarga will enable us to understand the socio-economic composition of the widows of city, but this is not sufficient to understand the process of integration of widows of the city. Analysis of the life of widows within family, neighbourhood and community is required to understand the integration of widows within Veerashaiva community. Hence, the researcher made an attempt to analyse the integration of widows within family, neighbourhood and community at large in the next chapter.

2.5 Every Day Life of Widows in Veerashaiva Community

Bereavement is a compound crisis even for a Veerashaiva widow. Immediate effect of widowhood is unbearable. The shock due to the unexpected death of the husband is very great. She is stunned and immobilised with extreme grief. She undergoes intense physical and emotional suffering, repeated feeling of helplessness and gloom which may sometimes lead to mental disorder. But this feeling could not live for longer period. After some time she gradually begins to participate in her every day activities. She can not be away for long from routine activities. By participating actively in her day-to-day activities she slowly starts forgetting her grief and loss sustained in her life.

The Veerashaiva family is a patriarchal family in which male members of the family exercise a greater control on family affairs. After the marriage a woman has to move to her husband's house and live with the members of the family of her husband. Even after the death of her husband, she is expected to live in the family of her in-laws.

The every day life of Veerashaiva widows of Gulbarga city has been observed at the time of field work. They get up early in the morning and take up household activities. First they wash the threshold of the main door and put vermilion to it. After that they have their bath and worship the 'Istalinga' an emblem of Shiva or symbol of knowledge. Before performing Linga pooja they do not take food and even water. After Linga pooja they take light tiffin or only a cup of tea or milk and attend the household duties. The widows who do not live with their in-laws cook the food for their children. They are being assisted by their children. The tasks attended by widows in joint families are different. They are required to work along with other members. There appears to be a kind of division of work among them. They serve the food first to the male members of the family and afterwards they take food along with the female members. In the afternoon they take rest for an hour or two and then engage themselves in other activities like cleaning the food grains and preparing the requirements which would supplement their daily consumption.

They are also found doing one or the other money generating activity. Sometimes they go in the evening to religious institutions called Mathas for attending religious discourses. Once a week they all gather in Matha and offer prayers by singing devotional songs. They feel that they get mental peace by attending these religious congregations. On certain auspicious occasions they perform the worship of deities like Mangalagouri, Sampath Shukravar, Varadashankar pooja in order to ensure merit and blessings of Gods and Godesses. They visit temple once in a week to have blessings of God. The religious institutions provide them an opportunity to come into contact with other women folk of the community. They share their sufferings and difficulties. It acts as a healing touch to their isolation.

Usually during the evening all the neighbours sit together and spend their time in gossiping. In course of gossiping they talk about the affairs of their kith and kin and near and dear relatives. They criticise the activities of other members of the family and society and exchange their joys and sorrows. Along with gossiping they are busy in doing one or the other works like stitching, cleaning and cutting the vegetables. Some elder widows take the role of guiding the younger generation quoting their experiences to them. They also impart moral values to the younger generation. A substantial number of widows are the members of Mahila Mandals. They know that undertaking the different cultural activities will improve the status and position of them.

There is a difference between educated employed widows and others as far as their day today life is concerned. A few of them are employed as teachers, peons, doctors and private employees. The widows who are working outside or on job complete their household duties in the early morning. They attend to their work and return home in the evening. In the evening they do the remaining household work, and relax for one or two hours. They see the TV programme for some hours for change and then they attend to their children. Again during night they prepare food for the members of the family. This is the only time available to them to discuss the family affairs. They make preparation to meet the needs of tomorrow. They spend their leisure time with their friends, neighbours and other relatives. During their holidays they see their relatives and attend some ceremonies.

REFERENCES

1. 1981 Census.
2. Mirza Mehdi Khan; 1981: Census of India, Vol. XXIII, Report, part-I, p. 73.

3. 1991 Census: Census of Gulbarga District.

4. Sadsivaiah, H.M. (Dr.): *A Comparative Study of Two Veerashaiva Monasteries*, pp. XVII. See also: Hastings James (Ed) 1953: *Encyclopedia of Religion and Ethics*, Vol. VIII, p. 69.

5. Srinivas, M.N. (Dr.): *Castes in Modern India*, p. 32.

6. Ishwaran, K. (Dr.): *Religion and Society Among the Lingayats of South India*, Vikas Publishing House, New Delhi, p. 2. See also; Parwathamma (Dr.) C.; 1972: *Sociological essays on Veerashaivism*; Popular Prakashan, Bombay, pp. 13.

3

Institutional Framework and Integration of Widows

In this chapter an attempt is made to study the process of integration of widows. The main focus in this chapter has been on the process of integration of widows within family and neighbourhood. Family, marriage and kinship constitute the elements of social structure of a society. They also have their corresponding institutions. In this study an attempt is made to study the phenomenon in its institutional framework. The structural functionalists have emphasized the institutional approach in understanding the social structure. Durkheim insisted that sociology as a science of society should study social facts that govern the institutional network in any social order. His ideas have been received well by other functionalists like Parsons and Merton. In this connection it is pertinent to mention the classification of institutions brought out by Talcott Parsons.

While discussing the social structure, Parsons attempted to define structure of institutions in terms of the patterned system of the social relationships of human beings. These institutions regulate and control the action of human beings in society. Parsons classified these institutions into three types namely, situational institutions, instrumental institutions and integrative institutions. Situational institutions are the organizations of roles about aspects of the situation in which actors and social systems are placed. Instrumental institutions are patterned about the attainment of certain goals as such and integrative institutions primarily oriented to regulating the relations of individuals, so as to avoid conflict or promote positive co-operation[1]. Stephan Mennell opined that the term social institutions has no precise and uniform usage. It is generally applied to aspects of social behaviour, regulated by well established, easily recognized and relatively stable norms, values and laws[2]. A few sociologists have identified family and kinship, economic, political and cultural institutions. Hence every human being leads a life within these institutional framework. The institution confers certain rights, responsibilities and privilegs on its members.

In this study it is intended to examine the process of integration of widows in the family, neighbourhood and community. Widowhood is the event which constitutes the greatest change in the family status of woman. The death of a spouse results in a major change in household structure. The widow is required to build her relationship with other family members in the absence of her spouse. For rebuilding the relations she takes a lot of time and needs some or the other type of support from family members, kinsmen, friends and neighbours. The sudden death of a spouse results in creating a great void in her life and the environment appears to her as hostile. She becomes depressed. It takes time to return to normalcy and integrate herself in the routine functioning of the family. In this task the size and the types of family organization play a vital role in society.

3.1 Integration of Widows Within the Family and Neighbourhood

Through its various agencies the society can be a source for providing services and economic supports for better integration of widows. The community often has numerous mechanisms made available to members to tide over the crises or problems in daily life. Employers, co-members of voluntary associations, neighbours and people who meet in a variety of circumstances can become resources for various supports and participation of widows in their life. One of the main resources can be the family, which can be defined along any lines, fictive or through marriage, biology or adoption as family can be particularly supportive if easily available. Sharing a complex household is inevitable and at times her separation may appear to be impossible. The Indian joint family though not as frequent as previously assumed, forms an interdependent unit, each member of which has definite rights and duties (Shah, 1974). Along with rights and duties each member has certain privileges and responsibilities. Even women have rights and responsibilities. However, it is difficult for widows to establish their rights but other members in the family may insist her to abide by the responsibilities.

The degree of disorganization of life produced by the death of husband depends on the degree to which he was an integral part of her life. In order to build a new life the widow must modify her old relationships and her life style. Voluntarily or not, she must make changes necessitated by the new situation. The new needs may dictate her to bring out new changes in her life. She is expected to be in the family, within the kin group and the neighbourhood. The reactions towards widows, of the members, kinsmen and neighbours would undergo certain modifications. She experiences a change in their attitudes towards her. Her rights and responsibilities are redefined. Her status varies with the type of family to which she belongs.

3.1.1 *Type of Family*

Broadly speaking there are two types of families in the Indian society. These are known as the joint and the nuclear family. Former is the traditional type of family which consists of members of at least three generations together. Majority of the Indian families, particularly in the countryside are of this type. The nuclear family consists of husband, wife and their unmarried children. Among Veerashaivas of Gulbarga we have joint families and nuclear families. The widows are found in both the types of families. In the Indian context it is very significant to know whether one is a member of joint family or nuclear family. The following table explains the type of family to which the widows belong.

Table 3.1
Distribution of Respondents Through Type of Family

SI. No.	*Type of family*	*Frequency*	*Percentage*
1	Joint family	157	62.8
2	Nuclear family	93	37.2
Total		250	100.0

Veerashaiva widows are classified under the category of family in which they are living. The data presented in the above table reveal that the highest percentage of widows belong to joint family. Of 250 widows 154 constituting 62.8% belong to joint families, while 93 constituting 37.2% reside in nuclear families. We may say that the joint families have been proved as safe place to live in with her changed status. The continuance of a majority of widows living in joint families for over a period of time speaks of the integration of widows in family. Participating in the day today activities in the family would ensure her integration. The data is significant in revealing the utility of joint living.

It is inferred from the data that low education level and economic dependency might have contributed to a large number of widows to stay in joint families. They appear to have integrated with them, despite the fact that they experience now and then difficulties of all kinds. The widows living in nuclear families are required to manage their affairs independently. They could live separately because their children are capable of earning. They may be separated from joint family.

3.1.2 Distribution of Widows by Their Present Settlement

The information pertaining to their present stay will help us to determine the status of widows within the family and participation of widows in household affairs. In this context we asked, "Where are you staying now?"

Table 3.2: Distribution of Respondents by Their Present Settlement

SI. No.	*Settlement*	*Frequency*	*Percentage*
1	Alone	20	8.0
2	Independently with small children	20	8.0
3	With adult non-earning children	30	12.0
4	With earning son(s)	127	50.8
5	With in-laws	11	4.4
6	With parents	14	5.6
7	With daughter(s)	22	8.8
8	With brothers	5	2.0
9	With sister(s)	1	0.4
Total		250	100.0

The data reveals that, after coming back of the widows to their normal life their settlement has changed. It is noticed that most of the respondents are staying with their earning children, where they are free from the burden of the family affairs, while 20 widows are staying alone. Among the widowed population, living alone is apparently a matter of choice and not the result of family rejection, indicating a congruence between family structure and family values (Lopata, 1971, 1973; Townsend, 1957; Troll,

1971; Tunstall, 1966). The table shows that, even widows are capable of leading an independent life after the death of their husbands. Nearly about 70% of them are with their children without moving towards anybody.

3.1.3 *Size of the Family*

Size of the family plays an important role in the living of an individual. It is always felt that greater the size of the family more secured are the members of it. The joint families have always stood for covering the risks of life. The widows living in large families overcome their grief by identifying themselves more and more with the inmates of the family. Widows are not thrown out to the problems of life. Joint families provided the needed support emotional and economic to the widows. It is therefore, not possible to provide a clear picture of the status of widows in Veerashaiva community. Also the widows in Veerashaiva community are not so much separated from the routine life owing to the beliefs brought to them by Veerashaivism. A Veerashaiva widow does not face all the tribulations of a widow of a twice born communities. The conditions created by Veerashaivisim are more favourable for a widow to overcome her crisis as compared to widows in other Hindu communities. Joint family is still a predominant feature of Veerashaivas in urban setting. The following table brings out clearly the situation in this respect.

Table 3.3

Distribution of Widows by Size of the Family

Sl. No.	*Household size*	*Frequency*	*Percentage*
1	Alone	17	6.8
2	Upto 5 members	120	48.0
3	6-10 members	97	38.8
4	11-15 members	14	5.6
5	16-20 members	2	0.8
Total		250	100.0

On the basis of above table we may distribute the

widows according to their family size. It can be revealed that, 6.8% (17) respondents are living alone, leading an independent life without depending on anybody, 48% (120) respondents are living with upto 5 members family, 38.8% (97) respondents are living with family size of 6-10 members, 5.6% (14) respondents are living with family size of 11-15 members, whereas 0.8% (2) respondents are living with family size of 16-20 members.

It is observed that nearly 86% of the widows come from the families which have 5-10 members. This reveals the fact that the widows do not appear to be going in for establishing their own families after the death of their husbands. They prefer to live with the families integrating themselves. It is significant to note that only 6.8% of the respondents live alone and lead the life of a widow. Security appears to be the main reason for their choice in living with the members of the families of their husbands.

3.1.4 *Attitude of Respondents Towards Remarriage*

One of the important objectives of our study is to ascertain the attitude of the Veerashaiva widows towards remarriage. It is very interesting to note that widow remarriage is not encouraged though is permitted by Veerashaivisim. A large number of widows showed their unfavourable attitude towards remarriage while a small number of them expressed their opinion in its favour. Among twice-born communities widow remarriage is prohibited. As early as 18th century the social reformers preached widow remarriage. Raja Ram Mohan Roy spearheaded the social reform movements in Bengal. The practice of child marriage resulted in making a large number of female children as widows. They were denied the most precious human rights, right to live. Atrocities on widows were severely condemned. The social reformers argued in favour of widow remarriage. The fact that Veerashaivism permitted widow remarriage is a single achievement in recognizing the principle of equality and liberation from the curse of widowhood. The women appeared to have enjoyed more freedom compared to others. The fact that only one case is accepted for remarriage, speaks of the attitude of women towards widow remarriage.

The reason, perhaps, appears to be the attitude of women towards the conception of life. In case of Veerashaivas it was observed that the atrocities on women were of lesser magnitude and certainly not hostile to better living. It is said that remarriage is not a solution to avert the crisis of the death of husband. An attempt is made to know the attitude of widows in respect of widow remarriage. Their responses are brought out in the table given below.

Table 3.4: Respondent's Attitude Towards Remarriage

Sl. No.	*Attitude*	*Frequency*	*Percentage*
1	Favourable	1	0.4
2	Unfavourable	249	99.6
Total		250	100.0

The above table depicts the respondents' attitude towards widow remarriage. The data revealed that 99.6% (249) of the respondents did not favour the idea of remarriage.

Only 0.4% (01) of respondents showed their favourable attitude. They felt that if suitable partner is available, remarriage can be considered. It is worth while to probe into their unfortunate attitude towards remarriage.

The Veerashaiva widows have explained the reasons for their continuing as widows. They gave different reasons, when individually they were contacted. A large number of them have stated that the love and respect for their deceased husbands and the fear of suffering of children if they are remarried, made them remain as widows. Among other reasons narrated are people's disrespect towards remarried widows and the adult children who are looked upon. The elders felt that the widow remarriage though permitted by the Veerashaiva community, the practice of it was not considered as a welcome. It appears that the other communities surrounding it restricted widow remarriage and this might have restricted many to reject it as a solution. It is interesting to note that whether a community permits or rejects, the effect is the same in respect of widow remarriage.

Widow remarriage has been viewed as a progressive measure by social reformers and social workers. They fought for its acceptance by the society and people. It may work out well when a widow has no issues. But for a widow with issues will be a problem to opt for remarriage. Such a situation may create several problems of adjustment with the new environment.

The study of A.P. Katti and H.V. Nagesh regarding the widows' willingness to remarry revealed that "about 97 per cent of rural Hindu widows and 92 per cent of Hindu widows in the urban area were not willing to remarry. Only three per cent of the rural Hindu widows and six per cent of urban Hindu widows were willing to remarry, inspite of the fact that a large proportion of them reported that their religion permitted it." The present study confirms such a view and also presents the reasons for not favouring it.

3.2 Interpersonal Relations of Widows in Family

In this part of the thesis, this study tries to analyse the various interpersonal relations of widows in family. It deals with the relations between wife and husband, wife and in-laws, wife and wife's parents. The interpersonal relations of widows with their husbands may be analysed in the following aspects.

3.2.1 Widows and Their Relation With Husbands

Marriage is a union of two souls. It is a union of husband and wife by sharing each other's joys and sorrows. They are required to work shoulder to shoulder in their every day living. The death of a spouse breaks this relationship and leads to a crisis of bereavement. The effect of widowhood depends on the type of relationship that they maintained with their husbands. The table given below describes the relationship of the respondents with their husbands. In order to measure the effect, an attempt is made to divide the respondents into four categories namely very good, good, bad and indifferent.

Table 3.5: Distribution of Respondents by Their Relation With Husbands

SI. No.	*Type of relationship*	*Frequency*	*Percentage*
1	Very good	28	11.2
2	Good	172	68.8
3	Bad	10	4.0
4	Indifferent	40	16.0
Total		250	100.0

The above table depicts the type of relations the widows had with their husbands. The highest percentage 68.8% (172) of widows maintained good relations with their husbands, the lowest percentage 4.0% (10) of widows maintained bad relations, whereas 11.2% (28) of widows maintained very good relations and 16% (40) widows maintained indifferent type of relations with their husbands.

It can be further inferred from the table that for 68.8% of widows, the death of the husband brings serious effect on them, because they maintained a good relations with them, while for 28 widows it is very serious crisis due to their very good relationship with their husbands. But for 10 widows the death of husbands has no serious effect because they did not maintain good relations and for 40 widows it has no serious impact due to the indifferent relations between them. This type of relation between husband and wife help for their integration in the family after the death of their husbands. It appears that among Veerashaivas the family life appears to be one of adjustment and not one of discard and unhappiness. It may be interpreted that there is the total subordination of women to male domination or to the acceptance of equality. The smoother relations between husband and wife depend on the educational status of the husband, occupation status of the husband and age gap between partners both at the time of marriage and at the time of his death. The relations between husband and wife may be more smooth in case the husbands are highly educated and engaged in well-yielding occupations. Sometimes the relations may be good among them who are qualified equally and holding equal occupation within the society. The relation between them also varies by age gap between them at the time of marriage and his death, the relations may be good and sometimes may not be good, due to variations in their way of thinking. Thus a big gap between marriageable age for men and women results in earlier widowhood for women. In our study the same situation is noticed. It results in creating the problems of integration and adjustment in family. They had to suffer for life-time both psychologically and financially since they lost their working partners.

The death of a husband brings in its trail a number of problems. The financial condition gets aggravated due to the sudden stoppage of husbands income. This leaves the widows at the mercy of the immediate group-family. This necessitates their dependence on others within the family. In order to ascertain the help received from the husband's family we asked a question, 'Did the elders in your husband's family provide help to you'? The below table depicts the help received from the husband's family.

Table 3.6: Did the Elders in Your Husband's Family Provide Help to You?

Sl. No.	*Response*	*Frequency*	*Percentage*
1	Yes	52	20.8
2	No	198	79.2
Total		250	100.0

From the table it can be inferred that, a majority of widows 79.2% (198) reported that they did not provide any type of help to them, where as 20.8% (52) widows stated that the elders of the husband's family came forward and provided help to them.

It is further clarified by knowing the reasons for not providing help to them and the help received from them was also studied. Among 250 respondents only 20 (52) percent received the help from husband's family. They reported that their families gave different types of helps like, shelter and financial support for fulfilling just demands and they showed sympathy towards them. They also reported that these different types of helps provided by them helped them for better integration within the family. But for a large number of widows integration became a problem and could not establish themselves for a considerable period of time. Nearly 79% (198) percent of widows explained various reasons for not receiving help from their husband's family. Some of the reasons mentioned by them are: *i)* children provided all kinds of help to them, *ii)* husband's family was divided even before their husband's death, *iii)* poor economic conditions of the husband's family, *iv)* economic conditions were good but the members had no sympathy towards them and wanted to sever relations from them. These reasons contributed towards creating problems to widows immediately after the death of their husbands.

The lack of support from their husband's family created a sense of insecurity among widows after the death of their husbands. In order to understand the state of insecurity faced by widows, we asked 'state the period you felt insecured'.

Table 3.7: Feeling of Insecurity After the Death of Their Husbands

Sl. No.	*Period*	*Frequency*	*Percentage*
1	1-3 years	37	14.8
2	4 - 6 years	21	8.4
3	7-9 years	2	0.8
4	10-12 years	2	0.8
5	13-15 years	7	2.8
6	Till now	36	14.4
7	No	145	58.0
Total		250	100.0

The above table depicts the percentage distribution of widows by their sense of insecurity after they lost their husbands. It is noticed that 14.8% (37) respondents felt in secured upto 3 years, 8.4% (21) felt upto 4-6 years, 0.8% (2) upto 7-9 years, 0.8% (2) felt upto to 10-12 years, 2.8% (7) felt upto 13-15 years, 14.4% (36) till, now they have a sense of insecurity, while 58% (145) did not feel insecure even after they lost their husbands. Among 145 widows those who felt insecured have given different reasons. Most of them did not feel insecure eventhough they lost their husbands, because they had security from their adult sons, few of them reported that they had security from parents, in-laws, co-wife, daughters, brothers, husband's property, and one respondent did not feel insecure as she had security from the employer of her husband. The sense of insecurity is more serious in the case of those widows whose husbands were employed in a well-paid jobs like doctors, engineers, accountants, clerks, teachers, police, drivers, etc., and on account of the loss of income due to the death of the bread-winner and absence of someone who gives shelter and support during widowhood it will be very serious.

The widowhood forces them to adapt to a life which would eventually make them suffer in their life and return to normalcy of life and living after a considerable period of suffering. In this context the present study tries to analyse the plans they have for their future for proper integration. Every widow is forced to have one or the other plan for future life in the absence of her husband. Because her main aim is to live with others and adjust with others in the most unfavourable moment of life. Among 250 widows (62) constituting 24.8% were found with some plan that could lead them toward a better living with their children. While some other widows have an idea of undertaking an income generating activity for leading a trouble-free life. This indicates that they intended to come to normal life situation by having some kind of income yielding activity. Even a few of them have an idea of continuing life with in-laws without establishing a separate house.

3.2.2 *Widows and Their in-laws*

The emerging phenomenon after the death of her husband is to opt for a new kind of life as imposed on her by the in-laws. The Veerashaiva widows of Gulbarga faced stiffness of the in-laws in respect of her living, decision making, moving out of the home and decisions in financial matters. The following table depicts the condition of the widows.

Table 3.8: Did You Undergo the Stiffness of Your in-Laws After Your Husband's Death?

Sl. No.	*Response*	*Frequency*	*Percentage*
1	Yes	224	89.6
2	No	26	10.4
Total		250	100.0

The statistical data presented in the above table depicts the percentage distribution of widows by undergoing stiffness of their in-laws after their husbands' death. The majority, 89.6% (224) of widows reported that they did undergo the stiffness of their in-laws after their husbands' death and the very lowest number 10.4% (26) of widows have not undergone the stiffness of their in-laws.

Those widows who have not undergone the stiffness of their in-laws, were helped by them in their day-to-day activities. Even most of them were advised by them for coming back to normal life. But a large number of them i.e. 89.6% were not free from such restrictions.

The widows felt the loss of authority and freedom. Restrictions on widows differ from one family to another. As most of the widows belonged to joint families, they experienced the stiffness of the attitudes of their in-laws. They narrated their difficult situations, which made them observe all the restrictions regarding moving out of the family, freedom in meeting others and taking the decisions about their children. From this state the widows have to move towards the normal life conditions. It required a great patience on the part of widows to be with their in-laws.

The Veerashaiva widows have mentioned the different categories of persons who advised them to come to normal life. A large number of (202) widows have stated that the neighbours have advised them for coming back to normal life, among others (120) widows were advised by parents, (70) widows were advised by their in-laws, and a few of them were advised by brothers, sisters, friends, religious priests, children and other relatives.

The stress and strain of transition is usually accompanied by feelings of loneliness, especially in the cases where the husband-wife relationship was cordial. "An early study of metropolitan Chicago widows brought forth numerous forms and components of loneliness (Lopata 1969, 1973). A widow can miss the late husband as a person unique and irreplaceable, an object of love, someone who loved her, a companion, an escort to public places, a partner in couple, companion at interaction, someone around whom time and work were organized, and just another presence in the home." Loneliness was to be felt for the whole life because a woman enjoyed while the husband was alive. The study of 250 widows reveals the loneliness of widows after their husbands' death. In strongly patriarchal societies the social isolation of the widow may be prevented by a guaranteed continuation of membership in the late husband's kin line (Phillips, 1953; Pauline, 1963). This loneliness of widows is a psychological feeling which is found among the widows for first few years. They feel that they have lost security and feel lonely on certain social contexts where both of them lived as partners in the work of family. In the initial period the Veerashaiva widows felt lonely when they were prohibited from attending certain auspicious functions. This type of feeling will not continue for longer period, as they come into contact with more and more number of persons who made them understand that the death of the husbands is a matter of fate and not of their own making. The table given below describes the feeling of loneliness among Veerashaiva widows.

Table 3.9: Distribution of Respondents by Their Sense of Loneliness

SI. No.	*Response*	*Frequency*	*Percentage*
1	Yes	112	44.8
2	No	138	55.2
Total		250	100.0

The percentage distribution of widows by their feeling of loneliness can be understood by the statistical data presented in the above table. It is noticed that 44.8% (112) widows feel lonely among their family members. It can be further inferred from the data that, nearly half of the widows dwelt lonely, because of the loss of companionship, loss of freedom, sense of dependency. Due to the inner feelings, for first few years they felt lonely. More than half i.e. 55.2%(138) of the respondents answered that they did not feel lonely among their family members. Because they were leading a life of widowhood for more than ten years.

Inspite of the grief and loneliness, the widow learns to live in a world without her husband. The task of developing new social roles and relations may also, however would be difficult. In this context it is necessary to know when the widows could resume their normal work after the death of their husbands.

Table 3.10: Distribution of Respondents by Resuming to Normal Work

Sl. No.	Period	Frequency	Percentage
1	After 3 months	112	44.8
2	After 6 months	43	17.2
3	After 9 months	3	1.2
4	After 1 year	68	27.2
5	After 2 years	17	6.8
6	After 3 years	4	1.6
7	After 4 years	1	0.4
8	After 5 years	1	0.4
9	Not yet	1	0.4
Total		250	100.0

It can be inferred from the table that/ majority of the widows resumed their work within 3 months after the passing away of their husbands. Nearly 90% of them returned to normal life after one year as a result of the advice of elder members of the family, friends, neighbours and children. A few widows reassumed their normal work within 8 days due to inevitable circumstances; Such a situation arises when there is no one to look after her children. She has to look for some kind of activity to maintain her day-to-day life.

3.2.3 *Immediate Reactions of In-laws Towards Widows*

The death of the husbands creates a considerable change

in the life of married women. The reactions of in-laws towards them after their husband's death is most important in understanding the integration of widows within the family. It may have favourable attitude towards them. They will help for better and sooner integration. In our study they have reported variety of reactions towards their husbands' death.

Table 3.11: Immediate Reaction of In-laws Towards Respondents

Sl. No.	Relations	Frequency	Percentage
1	Favourable	142	56.8
2	Unfavourable	25	10.0
3	Not applicable	83	33.2
Total		250	100.0

Information pertaining to the reactions of in-laws towards widows shows that, every widow has more than one reaction from her in-laws. Most of the in-laws' reactions towards her were sympathetic and they were found to be worried about their future. While very less number of widows hold the idea that, their in-laws have unfavourable attitude towards them, thinking that they were the cause for the death of their sons. Due to this, some in-laws send them towards their parent's family. In such cases the process of integration is very difficult and takes more time.

Those widows who have favourable reactions from in-laws helped them for better integration. A number of (56.8%) widows reported that, their in-laws worried very much for the loss of their son as well as the widowed life of their daughters-in-law. They provided guidance to their future life. This type of feeling towards widows is only for a few years, gradually they change their attitude towards them; this changing reactions of in-laws may be understood by asking, "What were reactions of in-laws towards the widows?" The table given below explains the situation.

Table 3.12: Reactions of In-laws Towards Respondents at Present

Sl. No.	Relations	Frequency	Percentage
1	Favourable	110	44.0
2	Unfavourable	45	18.0
3	Not applicable	95	38.0
Total		250	100.0

Comparing to immediate reactions of in-laws towards widows, 44% of the respondents made it very clear that they had received favourable treatment from in-laws after the death of their husbands. Only 18% of them stated they received unfavourable treatment from in-laws. But for 38% widows it is not applicable at present because their in-laws have ended their life both before and after their husband's death.

In general it is noticed that family members treat widows sympathetically or indifferently. Relatives seem to be more indifferent than family members. However, this sort of treatment is meted out more to the non-working widows.

3.2.4 Widow's Parents Relations

Family is regarded as a better tool for integration of widows. Like in-laws' family, the parental family also plays an important role in the process of integration. An inquiry into the reactions of parents towards widows for first few days reveals that largest number of them have received sympathetic treatment. The widows of modern times do not hesitate to seek the help from their parents.

This study also tries to analyse the reactions of parents towards widows at present. It can be noticed that a considerable number of widows have favourable attitudes from their parents. They reported that their parents were visiting them as their kith and kin. While very few widows reported that, their parents have unfavourable attitudes towards them. It is not applicable for merely half of the respondents, because their parents were not alive.

3.3 Role of Respondents in Family Before and After Widowhood

The integration of widows in family also includes the role of respondents in the family. Here an attempt is made to analyse the role of respondents in the family both before and after their widowhood. There are several set of duties assigned to women within the family. Their duties were performed with the co-operation of family members. From this study it can be inferred that almost all widows performed their role by doing household chores.

An analysis of the role of respondents in the family after widowhood shows that about 192 widows, play their role as household workers, 18 widows assist their mothers-in-law, 23 play their role by assisting their daughters-in-law. The widows numbering 14 who are living in their parents family, play their role by assisting their parents, 121 respondents stated that their role is to look after the children in the family, 3 widows assisted their co-wives, one of the most important roles that 37 widows are playing in their family is as a head of the family, while 113 respondents are playing other roles like helping their children, and doing one or other income generating activity to supplement the family income. Decisions are made by mutual consultations in all matters, since the children belong to an older age group. They have a major say in all matters pertaining to family. Working widows have to shoulder the family responsibility in addition to the office work. In the absence of their members of the family to discuss with, they often take decisions independently, but the non-working widows don't do so. However, wherever the scope for consultation is available they seem to take the opportunity. Thus the Veerashaiva Widows of Gulbarga are playing different roles in the process of integration.

3.4 Neighbourhood

A neighbourhood is viewed as physical neighbours have a sense of nearness, and interact socially. John McClaughly (1980; 369) defined the neighbourhood "as a predominantly residential area of a city that is characterised by its own economic, cultural and social institutions, typified by some traditions of identity and continuity and inhabited by people who perceive themselves to be residents of the neighbourhood and participants in its common life"[4]. The National Commission on Neighbourhoods (1979; 7) analysed, each neighbourhood is what the inhabitants that it is. The only genuinely accurate delineation of neighbourhood is done by the people who live there, work there retire there, and take pride in themselves as well as their community[5]. Albert Hunter (1974) referred neighbourhood as "symbolic communities". He described them as social objects with two main elements; cognition and sentiment. Sentiments reflect their attachment to the neighbourhood and their evaluation of its quality[6].

The widows of Gulbarga are living in social areas in which they must be able to regain earlier social relations or engage in new social roles if they are to avoid isolation. Unlike family contact, the neighbours may also help for integration of widows. It is said that contact with friends and neighbours may be subject to variation. Because they are not formally prescribed like kinship roles, relations which frequently decline when conditions arise which make interaction difficult. Friendships may decrease with age, loss of income or physical incapacity[7] (Shanas, 1962).

In middle age, friendship commonly develops around the work setting, through participation in voluntary organizations, or in the neighbourhood. The widow faces difficulty for developing friendship in the absence of her husband. Lopata (1973)[8] stresses the importance of peer support in helping the widow adjust to her bereavement. Generally, friendship and neighbourhood foster a kind of belonging based upon conviviality (Houchschild 1973)[9].

The following items are used to discuss integration of widows within neighbourhood. How many neighbours you know visit you? Did your neighbours visit you immediately after your husband's death? Did your neighbours visit you as frequently as before widowhood? Are you now getting any support from your neighbours? If yes, what type of support are you getting?

Comparing to family members, the neighbours are a better source of companionship for widow's participation in daily activities. It is necessary to know, how many neighbours they know, visit them for understanding their integration process. The table given below depicts the number of neighbours visiting the widows.

Table 3.13
How Many Neighbours You Know to Visit?

Sl. No.	*Response*	*Frequency*	*Percentage*
1	1-5 members	28	11.2
2	6-10 members	46	18.4
3	11 - 15 members	65	26.0
4	16-20 members	36	14.4
5	21-25 members	13	5.2
6	26 and above	62	24.8
Total		250	100.0

An analysis of the data shows that 11.2%(28) respondents have 1-5 neighbours to visit, 18.4%(46) have 11-15 neighbours. 14.4%(36) have 16-20 neighbours, 5.2%(13) have 21-25 neighbours, 24.8%(62) have 26 and above neighbours.

It can be further inferred from the data, that maximum number of respondents have upto 15 neighbours to visit them, and go for shopping, attend religious and social functions. These findings show that neighbours provide companionship and are able to share activity with the respondents.

In order to understand the type of relationship they maintained with their neighbours, we asked them a question 'Did your neighbours visit you immediately after your husband's death?'

Table 3.14: Distribution of Respondents by the Visits of Their Neighbours Immediately After the Death of Their Husband

SI. No.	*Response*	*Frequency*	*Percentage*
1	Yes	244	97.6
2	No	6	2.4
Total		250	100.0

The above table depicts the percentage distribution of widows by the visits of their neighbours immediately after the death of their husband. About 97.6% (244) widows reported that their neighbours visited them immediately after their husbands death. This shows that, the relation between respondents and their neighbours is favourable. And only 2.4% widows reported that, the neighbours did not visit immediately because his death occurred in a distant place. They may get social and emotional support from their neighbours.

3.5 Economic Participation of Widows and Family Organisation

Economic activity is treated as basic and important in all societies. It is defined differently by different social scientists. If some treated earning and producing food as an economic activity, the others treated it as any activity in which resources and skills are used by man to continue his existence in society. Still others feel the activities which are related to earning and/or disposing of wealth would come under the sphere of economic activity. However, we can state that in every society there is some trend of division of labour based on sex. In traditional India the tasks of women are rarely included in the category of economic activities. The traditional division of labour in India is based on sex. It is the men who can make earnings and women are supposed to look after the household activities.

The economic participation of widows in the family organisation is examined in the framework of division of labour on the basis of sex in the context of Veerashaiva community. The Veerashaiva women perform the household chores apart from undertaking varieties of supportive economic activities. Any supportive economic activity undertaken by them is an additional activity to the domestic work. The division of work on the basis of sex is still very significant. The widows are in no way different from other women in this respect. Most of the activities at home and outside tend to continue even after the death of husband.

If a widow has children to be brought up, she struggles to find out the means to earn livelihood. In this process, she bears an additional economic responsibility.

The psychological and emotional stress ,upon widowhood is not, however, the only component. Widowhood can be viewed as a complex transition, with multiple possible consequences, both subjective and objective. While both sexes can be expected to experience the subjective loss of partner and bereavement, the objective consequences differ somewhat for widows and widowers. The consequences of loss of spouse are, quite naturally some what differentiated between males and females due to gender roles and the sex-based division of labour in marriage (Atchley 1975)[10]. Further it is stated "women, within the traditional division of labour, have relied upon the husbands as providers of numerous services and of the major part of household income. Males in the traditional division of labour have lost the homemaking and child-care services provided by the wife. Apart from the problems of bereavement and subjective adaptation in widowhood, then, there are numerous objective changes and consequences which are thought to occur following loss of spouse and to which the widowhood must respond."[11]

Apart from the problems of bereavement the most frequently mentioned consequence for women is a serious decrease in family income precipitated by death of the husband, the major earner. Widows must make an adjustment to loss in income as well as loss of the person or their spouse. The death of the spouse results in changes in family composition and affects economic status of the household members. It leads to a serious decline in economic wellbeing for surviving of household members. Corcoran 1979; Holden, Burkhauser and Myers 1986; Hyman 1983; Morgan 1981; Zick and Smith 1983.

Financial stress would aggravate the psychological stress of bereavement, inhibit the widow's ability to undertake new social or recreational activities (Arling 1976)[12], or precipitate the additional adaptations to paid employment or residential relocation (Morgan 1979)[13]. The traditional division of labour, leaving wives financially dependent upon their husbands' earnings and provision for widowhood support, implied that the wife was subjected to a dramatic alteration of lifestyle upon the death of the spouse in the event that he had inadequately prepared for her security. In addition, many wives were feared to be unschooled in financial matters relating to the household (Lopata 1973)[14]. Although it would be anticipated that the situation is changing as increasing numbers of women are employed and become more active in the financial life of the family, males remain the major family earners (Morgan *etal* 1974)[15].

"Economic change, then, would seem to be one of the most predictable objective consequences of loss of spouse for women". When a woman loses her husband owing to death, she is likely to simultaneously experience a sharp drop in her standard of living. A number of studies indicate that widowed women become economically handicapped compared to those who have husbands. As compared to women having husbands widows experience more economic problems. The middle aged widows are less likely to go in for remarriage because they adjust with the family members by undertaking any economic role assigned to them. They do not undertake any economic activity that could make them independent. In addition, "being older and female in a world that values youth and maleness, may further hamper the middle aged women's ability to compete in labour market" (Bane 1975)[16].

Information on the economic status of widows is rather sparse; but it suggests a consistent pattern of poverty and deprivation. Lower family incomes for households headed by widows are regularly reported in survey research (Palmore et al, 1966; Lopata, 1973; Morgan, 1976; Steinhart, 1976; Walther and Morgan, 1978)[17]. Apart from attention to the amounts and adequacy of income in widowhood, a small amount of empirical work has examined the sources of income and how these change upon death of the husband. Since the income of the majority of households in this country still is derived from earnings of the male, hi£ death may be expected to remove this major source (Moran etal., 1974). This loss may be replaced by various sources of income. Thus previous studies of economic change at widowhood have suggested that the household economic status is disrupted in many ways upon loss of the husband. Loss of the primary breadwinner is assumed to result in a sudden precipitous loss of income and family standard of living. With the death of a spouse the household loses the labour income that the deceased may have provided plus the income from any assets that the deceased willed to individuals outside his or her immediate family (Cathleen D. Zick and K. R. Smith, 1988).

The death of husband creates several kinds of crisis in the family. Of them, the most significant is economic crisis. If there are no adequate resources at her command, she is required to take-up measures which could ensure adequate income to the family. Under the circumstances, a widow has three ways of tiding over the crisis namely: *i)* Various kinds of transfer of income like survivor benefits, *ii)* Other household members may increase their contributions to family income. For instance, a widow might move in with parents, in-laws or sister who works and shares expenses, *iii)* Mainly widowed women are supported by pensions, retirement plans, and social security benefits.

The widows in joint family may not find immediate need for earning and contributing to the economic resources of the family. But the situation differs in case of nuclear family. The widow is compelled to find out new ways to earn the resources. On this occasion she may need the support of her parents (if one surviving), kinsmen, neighbours and others. She is compelled to participate in economic activities. The widows who have the earning children, need not worry or hurry for a job. They may have to work more as additional responsibilities of managing the household are thrust on them. The study has clearly indicated that there is no such uniform behaviour which follows immediately after the death of their husbands. Much depends on the socio-economic and educational background of the family and the immediate needs of the family.

In the light of the above theoretical orientation of economic status of widows, in this study the economic participation of widows is understood in terms of role of widows immediately after the death of their husbands in respect of managing the economic affairs of the family. An attempt is made to take into account immediate dependence of widows, occupations before and after widowhood, the agencies that help the widows to overcome the situation, the problems faced before and after securing the new jobs. The job satisfaction, their income level, their economic relations with the family of husbands and parents and sources of economic support are examined.

Veerashaiva women are by and large dependent on their husbands. They are economically supported by them. The loss of husband, the main bread-winner creates a great void in the life of widows. The way widows manage this shock and crisis needs to be understood. It is observed that if a woman becomes a widow at young age the problems will be severe and in case a woman becomes a widow when her children are earning, the problems will be less severe. She may depend on her earning children. For a young widow, it will be really a problem and matter of choice and decision to seek the support from, either the parents or in-laws. On this occasion, the help from the brothers or sisters also can be sought.

Table 3.15: Immediate Dependence of Respondents

Sl. No.	*Response*	*Frequency*	*Percentage*
1	Parents	47	18.8
2	In-laws	43	17.2
3	Non-earning children	43	17.2
4	Earning children	96	38.4
5	Daughter(s)	7	2.8
6	Brothers	4	1.6
7	Sisters	1	0.4
8	Alone (herself)	9	3.6
Total		250	100.0

The above table shows that widows manage their economic problem by moving towards their kith and kin. About 47 (18.8%) widows moved towards parents, 43 (17.2%) widows stayed with in-laws, 43 (17.2%) non-earning children, whereas 96 (38.4%) stayed with earning children, 7 (2.8%) moved towards daughter(s) and 4 (1.6%) stayed with brothers and only one widow (0.4%) lived with sister and 9 (3.6%) widows depended on themselves.

It is inferred from the data that majority of (96) respondents reported that they did not feel insecure even after the death of their husbands due to the support from earning children. While very less number of (9) widows constituting 3.6% felt insecure due to immediate dependence on themselves. Also, it is inferred that

Veerashaiva community like other communities is kinship-bound and the traditional social order makes one to depend on kinsmen at the time of crisis.

For understanding widows occupational background and economic dependence, it is necessary to analyse and assess the nature of economic participation. It is extremely difficult to explain the economic contribution of women to a family. Most of her work is considered as non-economic. Many women do not have paid jobs. The data reveals that a large number of Veerashaiva women are working at home and do not undertake the remunerative jobs. Only a few of them who are educated and are pressed for economic earnings and have received training in professional courses have been earning members in their families. The table given below explains the occupational background of widows before widowhood.

Table 3.16

Occupation of Respondents Before Widowhood

Sl. No.	*Occupation*	*Frequency*	*Percentage*
1	Housewife	176	70.4
2	Land-labourer	46	18.4
3	Self-employed	7	2.8
4	Teacher	4	1.6
5	Private employer	15	6.0
6	Doctor	1	0.4
7	Govt. servant	1	0.4
Total		250	100.0

The statistical information pertaining to occupation of the respondents, before their widowhood shows that about 176 respondents were house wives, 46 were land-labourers, 7 were self employed, 4 were teachers, 15 were private employers, only one was doctor and one was Govt. servant. It can further be inferred from the table that a maximum number of widows constituting 70.4% were not at all engaged in any pile type of economic activity. This shows that among Veerashaivas male members have dominant place in economic activities, whereas 18.4% of them were working as land labourers even before their widowhood because of their poor family conditions, 2.8% widows were self employed in order to strengthen their economic conditions, 1.6% widows were teachers which helped them in all aspects of the family after their husband's death, 6% were private employers, which helped them to continue same even after widowhood, 0.4% was doctor with better economic position and 0.4% was Govt. servant who had better economic position within the family.

In this work the different occupations of widows are being studied. After becoming a widow whether it is necessary for her to take up any new occupation or continue to hold the same is studied. It is but natural to see that the widows were already in government service and were managing private business continued their occupation. Also, the agricultural labourers continued their work on the fields. The traditions are still very strong. The crisis may be overcome in the traditional way i.e. by shifting her dependence from husband to other kith and kin. There may be very few opportunities for them to go out of the family bonds and take up independent positions. The following table depicts the occupational changes occurred after widowhood.

Table 3.17

Occupation of Respondents After Widowhood

SI. No.	*Occupation*	*Frequency*	*Percentage*
1	House wife	168	67.2
2	Coolie or servant	46	18.4
3	Peon	10	4.0
4	Teacher	5	2.0
5	Doctor	1	0.4
6	Lecturer	1	0.4

7	Aya	5	2.0
8	Tailor	4	1.6
9	Vegetable seller	2	0.8
10	Dairy farming	1	0.4
11	Shop keeper	1	0.4
12	Managing the field	2	0.8
13	S.D.C.	2	0.8
14	Coconut seller	2	0.8
Total		250	100.0

Most of the respondents were engaged in one or the other occupation after their widowhood for their livelihood., The above table depicts the occupational background of widows after their widowhood. However, fourteen occupations are reported by the respondents. It is evident from the table that about 168 (67.2%) widows are not engaged in any type of job, they lead a dependent life as a householder, 46 (18.4%) widows are coolies and 10 (4.0%) widows are peons, 5 (2.0%) widows are working as teachers, only one (0.4%) widow is doctor and one widow (0.4%) is performing her dirty as lecturer, 5 (2.0%) widows are ayas, 4 (1.6%) widows started doing a job of tailor for their livelihood, 2 (0.8%) widows performing a business of vegetable selling, one (0.4%) is dairy farmer, one (0.4%) is running a small kirana shop, 2 (0.8%) widows are managing their field as the duty of their husbands, 2 (0.8%) widows are engaged in their husbands job as second division clerks, and 2 (0.8%) are doing a business of coconut.

From the table given above, it is clear that a Veerashaiva widow is not ordinarily required to go in for earning immediately after the death of her husband. A very few women have to find out new ways to meet the exigencies of life after the loss of their husbands' earning. The data revealed that only 4% of the widows have taken up the job of peons in order to support the family. A few of them have taken up to selling goods in order to make a living. But 67.2% of them did not feel any need for taking up new occupation. They were still doing household work. They were supported by the kith and kin.

A question was asked to those widows who have taken up new jobs and struggled to face the economic problems of the family. It is intended to know the persons who support them at the time of crisis. Of the 250 respondents 204 have not tried for any new economic venture as they continued the same. 46 respondents constituting 18.4% have struggled to take up new occupations to overcome the economic difficulties. The following table depicts the situation clearly in terms of persons who extended their help in new occupations.

Table 3.18: Help Received from Others in Securing a Job After the Death of Husband

Sl. No.	*Response*	*Frequency*	*Percentage*
1	Parents	4	8.69
2	Parents-in-law	2	4.34
3	Brothers	4	8.69
4	Friends	11	23.90
5	Neighbours	6	13.00
6	Husband's employers	3	6.50
7	Others	16	34.7
Total		46	100.0

The table above indicated that 8.69% (4) widows got help from their parents, in the case of 4.34% (2) widows parents-in-law helped for getting a job. 8.69% (4) got help from their brothers, 23.9%(ll) got help from friends, 13% (6) got help from their neighbours, 6.5% (3) got help from their husband's employer, whereas 34.7% (16) got help from their relatives for getting job. It can be further inferred from that about 204 widows were not at all doing any job, because they had support from the members of their family and property left by their husbands.

After their widowhood, the widows faced one or the

other problem for getting job. The table given below depicts, whether they faced problem.

Table 3.19

Did You Face Any Problem in Getting the Job?

Sl. No.	Response	Frequency	Percentage
1	Yes	11	23.9
2	No	35	76.1
Total		46	100.0

From statistical data it can be inferred that among 46 widows engaged in job after their widowhood, 23.9 % (11) widows answered that, they faced a problem of getting the job, whereas 76.81 % (35) widows opined that they did not face any problems to get themselves engaged in one or other job. It can be further inferred from the table that a maximum number of widows did not face any problems at all because they got one or the other type of help from their kith and kin. As most of the widows were illiterate they faced problems in getting the job. The table given below shows the reasons for facing the problems.

Table 3.20: Reasons for Facing the Problems in Getting the Job

Sl. No.	Reasons	Frequency	Percentage
1	Lack of proper education	9	81.8
2	Lack of proper experience and training	10	90.9
3	Lack of proper guidance and help	9	81.8

Among eleven widows, those who have faced problems in getting a job have given a number of reasons. The above table shows that about 81.8%(9) widows faced problems due to lack of proper education, whereas 90.9% (10) widows faced problems due to lack of proper experience and training whereas 81.8% (9) widows also faced a problem due to lack of proper guidance and help.

Even though the respondents engaged in one or the other income-generating activity, they were not satisfied with their job. They felt very bad about their poor condition. The following question is asked to the respondents to get an information about the job satisfaction. Are you satisfied with your present employment?

Table 3.21: Distribution of Respondents by Their Job Satisfaction

SI. No.	*Response*	*Frequency*	*Percentage*
1	Yes	60	73.2
2	No	22	26.8
Total		82	100.0

Among 250 widows 82 were engaged in one or other job. Among 82 widows 36 widows were engaged in a job even before their husbands' death. About 73.1% widows are satisfied with their present job, whereas 26.8% widows are not satisfied with their job, because of insufficiency of their earning and more number of dependants on them, Because of this dissatisfaction from job and insufficient earning they sought a financial help from different means when they were in need of it.

Table 3.22: Financial Help Received From Others After the Death of Husband

SI. No.	*Financial support from*	*Frequency*	*Percentage*
1	Family	174	69.6
2	Government	48	19.2
3	Husband's department	3	1.2
4	Community .	12	4.8
5	Not applicable	13	5.2
Total		250	100.0

The above table shows that 174 (69.6%) widows are getting financial support from family which is the basic institution of human society. About 48 (19.2%) widows are getting help from Government in the form of widow pension, 03 (1.2%) widows are getting help from their husbands' department, 12 (4.8%) are getting help from their nearers and dearers of the community and 13 (5.2%) widows donot take financial help from anybody because they have no need of it.

It can be further inferred that a maximum number of widows are getting help from their parents and parents-in-laws' family. This seeking of financial support shows that the death of the husband leads to a financial problem the husband being the major earner of the family.

In order to ascertain the economic status of the respondents family, the information pertaining to source and amount of income before their widowhood is essential. Because, before their widowhood, their husbands were main bread winner. Even the economic condition of the family also depends on their income. Hence, particulars regarding respondents' family income before widowhood were collected and same are presented below.

Table 3.23: Respondents' Family Income Before Widowhood

Sl. No.	*Income*	*Frequency*	*Percentage*
1	Up to Rs. 3600 per year	44	17.6
2	Rs. 3601 to 10000 per year	60	24.0
3	Rs. 10001 to 20000 per year	62	24.8
4	Rs. 20001 to 30000 per year	39	15.6
5	Rs. 30001 to 40000 per year	14	5.6
6	Rs. 40001 to 50000 per year	8	3.2
7	Rs. 50001 to 60000 per year	8	3.2
8	Rs. 60001 and above per year	15	6.0
Total		250	100.0

An analysis of the source and amount of income before widowhood reveals that 21.6 % (54) widows' family income per annum is Rs. 3600, 27.2 % (68) respondents' family income is Rs. 3601 to 10,000 p.y. 20.8 % (52) respondents belong to the income group of Rs. 10,001 to 20,000 p.y., and 12.4 % (31) respondents' income group is Rs. 20,001 to 30,000, 5.6 % (14) widow's family income by all sources is Rs. 30,001 to 40,000, whereas 3.2 % (8) widows' family income per annum is Rs. 40,001 to 50,000, while 3.2 % (8) widow's belong to income group of Rs. 50,001 to 60,000, and 6 % (15) widows' family income per year is Rs. 60,001 and above.

It can be inferred from the table that a good percentage is in the low income group that is 41.8, while 46 are in middle income group and remaining 12.4% widows are in high income group.

3.5.1 Respondent's Family Income After Widowhood

As regards the present source of income, it is seen that the majority of the respondents have joined the work force after the death of their husbands and are therefore solely dependent on their own income for their livelihood and for the maintenance of their families. Those respondents who are not working at present, their major sources of income are those of their children, husbands' pension, inherited property and a combination of all other sources. The table given below depicts the respondents' family income after widowhood.

Table 3.24

Respondents Family Income After Widowhood

SI. No.	*Income of the family*	*Frequency*	*Percentage*
1	Up to Rs. 3600 per year	35	14.0
2	Rs. 3601 to 10000 per year	68	27.2
3	Rs. 10001 to 20000 per year	59	23.6
4	Rs. 20001 to 30000 per year	36	14.4
5	Rs. 30001 to 40000 per year	11	4.4
6	Rs. 40001 to 50000 per year	8	3.2
7	Rs. 50001 to 60000 per year	9	3.6
8	Rs. 60001 and above per year	24	9.6
Total		250	100.0

As compared to the earlier economic condition of

widows, we do not find considerable change in the financial condition of the family, because one or the other person of the family is contributing to the financial condition of the family and even most of the widows started doing the job of their husbands. An analysis of the source and amount of income after widowhood reveals that, 35 (14%) respondents' annual income is upto Rs. 3600. 68 (27.2%) widows family income both before and after widowhood is Rs. 3601-10,000 per year, 59 (23.6%) widows come under income group of Rs. 10,001-20,000 per year, 36 respondents belong to the income group of Rs. 20,001 to 30,000 per year. 11(4.4%) widows family income per annum is Rs. 30,001 to 40,000, 8 (3.2%) widows belong to the income group of Rs.40,001 to 50,000, while 9 (3.6%) widows income group is Rs.50,001 to 60,000 per annum and 24 (9.6%) respondents belong to income group of Rs.60,001 and above.

The above data reveal that 41.2% are in low income group, while 42.4% belong to middle income group and 16.4% belong to high income group.

An analysis of the family income of the widows shows that most of the widows both before and after their widowhood belong to the middle income group.

The financial condition of widows includes the share in property that they got from their parents and husband's family. In order to ascertain the information about the share in the property that they had from the natal and marital family the following question was asked. Have you been given a share in the property of Natal and Marital family?

Table 3.25: Having Share in the Property of Natal Family

Sl. No.	*Share*	*Frequency*	*Percentage*
1	Yes	30	12.0
2	No	220	88.0
Total		250	100.0

The above table indicates that a majority of (220) widows do not have any share in their natal family. Only a less number of widows (30) get share in their natal family in the form of Agricultural Land, House, Money Jewellery/Shops, etc.,

Table 3.26: Having Share in the Property of In-laws' Family

Sl. No.	*Response*	*Frequency*	*Percentage*
1	Yes	167	66.8
2	No	45	18.0
3	There is no property at all	38	15.2
Total		250	100.0

An analysis of the widows' share in their marital family shows that a majority of (167) widows get their husbands' share in the property in the form of agricultural land, house, money, jewellery etc., While 45 widows have not received any share in the property of their marital family. Among 45 widows, 3 widows hold the property in common, and for 38 widows there is no property at all and there is no question of having share in it.

3.5.2 Widowhood and Support Systems

A woman influences the degree in disorganization of her life frame-works with the death of her husband. The society and the community in which she is located provide her with varying degrees of choice, the social roles, support systems, life style and self concept which form her life framework to come out of mourning and grief. A major part of life frameworks are the support systems. Resources in the form of people and various other social units can be pulled into a support network with whom supports can be exchanged. A support system is defined as a set of actions or objects which the giver or receiver or both define as necessary or helpful in maintaining a style of life (Lopata, 1971,a)[18]. The support systems are economic, service, social and emotional.

Widowhood and Economic support

The economic support system includes gifts of money, food or clothing or help with the payments for their objects and payment or help with the payments for rent or mortgage and for other bills such as medical expenses. In order to collect the source of economic support the following question was asked to widows. Who is giving the support? The reactions to the question are tabulated below.

Table 3.27: Source and Economic Support

SI. No.	*Source of support*	*Frequency*	*Percentage*
1	Parents in-law/brothers in-law	25	10.0
2	Parents	69	27.6
3	Brothers	9	3.6
4	Earning children	181	72.4
5	Neighbours	13	5.2
6	Others	41	16.4
7	No one	1	0.4

An analysis of the economic support shows that 25 widows are receiving economic support from parents-in-law /brothers-in-law, for 69 widows parents are providing the economic support, 9 widows are getting it, from brothers, a majority of (181) widows are receiving economic support from earning children, 13 widows are receiving from their nearers and dearers and only one widow has no need of any type of economic support from any source.

Source of Service Support

The service system includes provisions of transportation or legal aid, help in making major decisions, care during illness, childcare, minor household repairs and help with housework, shopping etc. The source of the service support is shown in table given below.

Table 3.28: Source of Service Support

Sl. No.	*Source of support*	*Frequency*	*Percentage*
1	Parents in-law/brothers in-law	52	20.8
2	Parents	73	29.2
3	Brothers	8	3.2
4	Earning children	199	79.6
5	Neighbours	15	6.0
6	Others	43	17.2
7	No one	1	0.4

An analysis of the source of economic support shows that 52 widows receiving service support from parents-in-law/brother-in-law. 73 widows are receiving from parents, 8 widows are receiving from children, 15 widows are receiving from neighbours, 43 widows are receiving from their other nearers and dearers and only one widow is not receiving from any body and there is no need of it for her.

Social Support and Widowhood

Social support system includes going with 'people to public places such as movies, entertaining, going out to lunch, going to temples celebrating festivals and other social activities mentioned by the respondent, in answer to an open-ended question. The same is presented below.

Table 3.29: Source of Social Support

Sl. No.	*Response*	*Frequency*	*Percentage*
1	Parents in-law/brothers in-law	41	16.4
2	Parents	103	41.2
3	Brothers	13	5.2
4	Children	197	78.8
5	Neighbours	210	84.0
6	Others	195	78.0

The above table depicts the source of social support for widows. Parents-in-law/brothers-in-law were providing one or the other social support for 41 widows, parents were providing for 103 widows, brothers were helping in one way or the other to 13 widows, children were providing social support for 197 widows while 210 widows are receiving social support from neighbours and 195 widows are receiving social support from friends, other relatives and their nearers and dearers. Thus an analysis of the social support shows that every widow is receiving social support from more than one source.

Emotional Support and Widowhood

The emotional support system is focussed on relational sentiments. We asked a widow to whom she feels closest, whom she most enjoys being with, to whom she tells her problems and who comforts her, to whom she turns in a crisis.

Table 3.30: Source of Emotional Support

Sl. No.	Source of support	Frequency	Percentage
1	Parents in-law/brothers in-law	36	14.4
2	Parents	105	42.0
3	Brothers	8	3.2
4	Children	196	78.4
5	Neighbours	214	85.6
6	Others	186	74.4

The extended kinship network, relatives and neighbours other than parents and children appear even in emotional support systems of Veerashaiva widows of Gulbarga city. Table 3.30 depicts the source of emotional support for widows, among 250 widows 36 widows were providing emotional support by parents-in-law, and 105 widows getting from parents, 8 widows from brothers and 196 widows were turning towards children for emotional support. 214 widows towards neighbours and 186 widows towards other relatives, friends and nearers and dearers.

The total number of current support system available to the widows in the present study includes the social support for 182 widows, emotional support for 198 widows, financial support for 25 widows and service support for 7 widows, and various economic benefits from Government.

Table 3.31: Distribution of Respondents by Receiving Benefits from Government

Sl. No.	*Benefits received*	*Frequency*	*Percentage*
1	Family benefits	21	8.4
2	Life insurance	6	2.4
3	Survivor benefits	21	8.4
4	Widow pension	30	12.0
5	Others (GPF)	2	0.8
6	No benefits	170	68.0
Total		250	100.0

Data pertaining to the benefits received from Government immediately after the death of their husbands shows that the majority of the respondents (68%) did not receive any benefits from Government because their husbands were not Government servants, while 8.4% (21) widows received family benefits, 2.4% (6) respondents received life insurance benefits, 8.4% (21) received survivor benefits, 12% (30) received widow pension, 0.8% (2) widows received other benefits like GPF through which the respondents were in a position to solve their immediate problems.

The death of a husband breaks up the pattern of engagement in the life of the wife in varying degrees and ways, this death creates a number of problems. Due to the loss of the major earner of the family the expenditure of family automatically decreases. In order to ascertain the answer about the cuts in family expenditure the following question is asked. Are there any drastic cuts in your expenditure after death?

Table 3.32: Cuts in Expenditure After Widowhood

Sl. No.	*Response*	*Frequency*	*Percentage*
1	Yes	195	78.0
2	No	55	22.0
Total		250	100.0

From this table it has been observed that about 195 (78%) widows' family expenditure was cut down drastically due to the loss of major earner of the family while 55 (22%) widows reported that there were no cuts in expenditure of family as compared to earlier life. This shows that his death affected the financial conditions of larger families.

3.6 Religion and Integration of Veerashaiva Widows in the Community

Every society has devised certain mechanism to facilitate the performance of its routine activities. They can be seen active within the institutional frame work. Women are considered as custodians of customs, beliefs, traditions, norms and values. They are regarded as rigid and traditional. The cultural themes are transmitted from generation to generation by them. The social, economic, educational and religious institutions influence the functioning of individuals. Of them religious institutions occupy a significant place in the role of performance of women as wives, mothers and daughters.

Religion is the human response to the apprehension of some thing, or power, which is supernatural and suprasensory. It is the expression of the manner, and type of adjustment effected by a people with their conception of the supernatural. This conception of the exact nature of the supernatural differs from society to society and people to people. Anthropologists treated religion as "any set of attitudes, beliefs and practices pertaining to supernatural power, whether it be forces, gods, spirits, ghosts, demons or any other imagined power"[19].

Some form of religion is found in all societies which meets certain individual and social needs. The functions of religion have been explained by Malinowski and Radcliffe Brown. Malinowski pointed out that "religion is intimately connected with various emotional states, which are states of tension. Similarly, hatred, greed, anger, love, etc, may rise due to various situations in man's life. These situations create stresses and strains and if permitted to exist over a long period of time frustrate all action. A human being has to be an acting individual and normal action is not possible in an emotionally upset state of existence. In such a situation, religion is used as a tool of adaptation; its purpose is to purge the human mind of its stress and strain. In other words, religion has the function of bringing about a readjustment between man and the supernatural in upset state of existence. It is a device to secure mental and psychical stability in an individual's life"[20]. As far as the function of religion is concerned Radcliffe Brown stated "it is not to purge fear and other emotional strains from the human mind, but to instil a sense of dependence on it. Brown opined that, ultimately the survival of the group is more important than that of the individual; and if the latter has to make some sacrifices it is in his own interest to do so, because without social survival individual survival is not possible"[21].

In every society religion helps to make man free from stress and strains and build the confidence with him. Like all other persons undergoing stress and strain, widows undergo mental crisis and loss of status. It is observed that a number of widows in Lingayat community feel a sense of hopelessness and dependency after the death of their husbands. Their kith and kin, neighbours, and other members of the community repeatedly define the situation in terms of the will or wish of God. They are being consoled by depicting the event and make them believe that none other than lord is responsible. They are advised to keep faith in the supernatural and look to their future by contributing their mite for the growth of children and/or other members of the family. The repeated mentioning of it to the widows would definitely lead to the release of stress and strain. The acceptance of religious dogmas and beliefs may make them forget gradually the tension, stress and strain. "Man-supernatural relationship is universal in all cultures. In the lives of all people, incidents do take place which defy logic and which the known laws of science cannot explain"[22].

In an appraisal of the position of women in Hindu civilization, Altekar (1958,194) opined, "In the present age when religion is gradually losing its hold on popular mind, the subject may appear as of no great importance to some of our readers. The case, however was quite different in the past. Religious rites and privileges were valued most highly, even political and proprietary rights faded before them in importance. The social status of an individual was vitally connected with the place which religion accorded to him in its rites and rituals. Privileges accorded or denied to women by religion will, therefore, throw valuable light on their position in society. In this early history man is seen excluding woman from religious services almost everywhere because he regarded her as unclean, mainly on account of her periodical menstruation. During this period the woman was the object of the greatest dread. The case is on record of an Australian aborigine going stark mad because he had unknowingly touched the blanket used by his wife during her period, and then killing first his wife and then himself under the influence of his frenzy. The dread which Australian felt was shared by the average man in his early history, when he did not know the physiological causes of the mysterious phenomenon, which he feared so much"[23].

Sociologically speaking, religion is system which regulates the lives of its adherents, ordinarily, people are attracted by a religious doctrine for certain mundane considerations, and not by its great ideas,. They hold a belief that by following certain religious principles, they may have a happy and prosperous life on earth. They are particularly influenced by the magical aspects of religious doctrines. Their belief in religion is motivated by economic-ethics.

India is rightly hailed as the land of many religions. Among them Veerashaivism is an important religion which has its adherents concentrated in Karnataka and spread out in other States of India. In Gulbarga Veerashaivas are very prominent in all walks of life. Though this faith existed from time immemorial, it achieved a great success in 12th century when Basaweshwara launched a very progressive movement in order to bring equality in society and make people liberated from the domination of rituals. As a result of it, a large number of socio-economic reforms were initiated. It is needless to mention that this revolution had its far-reaching impact on Indian culture.

Veerashaivism has gained importance as a protest movement against ritualism and Hindu Polytheism. It believes in monotheism, and preaches equality of all occupations. Today the Lingayats from the largest single community of Karnataka, which does not believe in Varnashrama Dharma, excessive ritualism and the Hindu theory of *Panchasutakas* (five pollutions) namely, *Janma* (birth), *Jati* (caste), *Rajaswa* (menstruation), *Ucchista* (remnants), *Mrityu* or *preta* (death)[24].

The Lingayats are also known as Lingawants, Lingangis, Sivabhaktas, and Vira-saivas. They derive their name from the Sanskrit word *Linga,* the phallic emblem, with the affix *ayata,* and are the people who wear the Linga habitually. Their name literally describes them; for the true Lingayat wears on his body a small silver box containing a stone phallus, which is the symbol of his faith and the loss of which is equivalent to spiritual death. The emblem is worn by both sexes. The men carry the box on a red silk scarf or a thread tied round the neck, while women wear it inside their costume, on a necktstring.

When working, the male wearer sometimes shifts it to his left arm.

A study of religions of the world reveals that the religious faiths evolved out in two forms. In the first form, the religions evolved through natural inherent urges and in the second form they were founded and patronised by a single person. Those religions which were born naturally are as old as the existence of humanity on this earth, they are the treasure-house of universal truths and a unique contribution of great experience of humanity. Those religions which are born naturally have given man religious freedom and opportunities to develop his personality and nature. The religions evolved naturally gave man the right to select the best possible values for his life and give up those values which were supposed to be outdated. This is the greatest cultural heritage endowed by natural religions. Such great cultural heritage is possessed by Shaiva and Veerashaiva religions.

In Veerashaiva Philosophy, *Ashtavarana, Panchachara* and *shatsthala* have got significance because *Ashtavarana* has been taken as eight aids of the faith. *Panchacharas* have been taken as five disciplinary practices and *Shatsthala* has been considered as union of *Anga* with *Linga* i.e., 'Linganga samarasya', in six stages. The most important ceremony of all Lingayats is known as the *astavarana,* or the eightfold sacrament. It is commonly asserted nowadays by prominent members of the Lingayat community that the true test of the Lingayat is the right to receive the full *astavarana,* and that the possession of a few of these eight rites only does not entitle the possessor to be styled a member of the community. The *astavarana* consists of eight rites known as *Guru, Linga, Jangam, Vibhuti, Rudrakshi, Mantra, Tirth, Prasad.* Lingayats will combine the worship of the special objects prescribed by Basava with the worship of purely Hindu deities such as Hanuman, Ganapathi, Ambabhavani, Veerabhadreshwar, Yellamma and many others.

The basic principles of Veerashaivism are Kayaka, equality, politeness, non-violence, humanity, co-ordination, Monotheism, universal brotherhood, Dashoha etc. *Shaktivishistadwaita* is the philosophy of Veerashaiva religion, which includes three concepts of Jeeva, Shiva and Shakti. The union of shakti-oriented Jeeva and shakti-oriented Shiva is called *Shaktivishistadwaita*. The *Lingangsamarasya* i.e., the union of individual soul with super soul Anga with Linga, Jeeva with Shiva is the end of life for Veerashaivas.

From the stand-point of Veerashaivism the Veerashaiva women were to be segregated neither temporarily nor permanently from the routine life. They were never considered inauspicious for religious activities or inferior in any of the day to day social activities. The fact that they are allowed to perform the pooja of their istalinga even when they undergo the monthly cycle, would make us understand that they are not barred from religious activities.

3.6.1 Religious Participation and Widows

The individuals participate in different activities in their day to day living. Religious activities are very significant for an individual as they facilitate in maintaining his identity in the community. Whether man, woman or widow, all participate in religious activities. They are centred around the religious dictates, beliefs and rituals. An important aspect of the study of religious life of individuals is their awareness to the philosophical tenants of the religion. Beginning with the worship of Istalinga of a Veerashaiva widow, we notice innumerable religious activities in which she participates. It is observed that certain principles are observed as rituals while others appear to be not known to her. Whether the knowledge of Astavarana, Panchachara and Satasthala is available to every individual or whether every one practises them in her daily life is a matter of great significance for a student of Veerashaiva society. For ordinary men the knowledge of rituals is more than the knowledge of their meanings. Therefore, we notice the widows get up in the morning and take their bath. After that they worship istalinga and undertake the routine work. Vibhuti is on their forehead. Istalinga is worn on their bodies. In case there are facilities available, they listen to religious discourses. The Veerashaiva widows perform these rituals every day and devote their time to household activities. Since they do not believe in pollution, they consider themselves on par with men in this respect. A question was asked to the veerashaiva widows about their performance of Istalinga worship every day even when they here in menstruation period. The following table depicts the situation.

Table 3.33: Performance of Lingapooja by Respondents During Menstrual Period

Sl. No.	*Response*	*Frequency*	*Percentage*
1	Yes	235	94.0
2	No	15	6.0
Total		250	100.0

The above table depicts the performance of Linga Pooja by widows during their menstrual period. The data reveals that 94% i.e., (235) of widows perform Lingpooja even during their menstrual period, and a few respondents i.e., (15) 06% of widows do not perform Linga Pooja during menstrual period. The widows believe that they wear linga on their bodies and hence no pollution. It is also believed that Linga has power of purification of the body. There is nothing like impure for a lingayat. It is said by some that if pollution is not observed snakes and scorpions will appear in their house. Such persons were believing Ambabhavani, Veerabhadreshwar, Ratagal Revanasiddeswar etc., as their family deities, they must be pure and clean and one required to take purity and pollution concept.

Apart from Linga Pooja Veerashaiva women worship

various deities in the form of worshipping saints, sadhus, Tapaswis, observe Vratas, Upavasa and perform various specified poojas. The form of worship may differ from woman to woman. Because the worshipping deities is an innate quality of every human-being. In this regard we asked a question to the respondents, "what is the purpose of performing various religious rituals?" Most of the (98%) widows opined that the loss of a spouse created a lot of problems and in order to be free from them the deities were worshipped while (2%) of widows opined that, they worshipped only for their mental satisfaction.

In order to understand the intensity of their worship we asked one more question whether their belief in religious practices changed after the death of their husbands. 87.2% (218) of the widows opined that their purpose of performing religious practices did not change but for 12.8% (32) widows their purpose of performing the religious practices changed after their husbands' death, because they experienced an irreparable loss.

Veerashaivas do not distinguish between man and woman in religious matters. They regard woman as having equal religious status. They do not put restrictions on the performance of religious rituals even after their widowhood. Sometimes they will start performing more rituals after their husbands' death. The table given below depicts the worship of deity by the respondents even after their widowhood.

Table 3.34: Worship of Deities After Widowhood

Sl. No.	*Response*	*Frequency*	*Percentage*
1	Increased	46	18.4
2	Decreased	34	13.6
3	Remained same	170	68.0
Total		250	100.0

The above data shows that the worship of God for 68% (170) widows remained same as before widowhood, whereas for 18.4% (46) widows it has increased and for 13.6% (34) widows decreased. It can be further inferred that the majority of the Veerashaiva widows continued their religious practices, as in earlier days and only for 13.6% of widows the worship of supernatural forces decreased due to the unexpected event in their life. And they also opined that, when they lost their God (husband) what was left for them to worship. Not only they stopped worship of deity but also they stopped performing the prayers on all occasions. Like other communities Veerashaiva community also offers prayers to several Gods and Goddesses. They visit several temples like, Sharanabasaveshwara Temple, Hanuman temple, Basavanna temple, Ambabhavani temple, Raghavendra temple, Veerabhadreshwar temple, etc. It is observed that Veerashaivas worship a large number of deities even when Veerashiva religion attaches a greater significance to monotheism. Here we notice the difference between theory and practice in respect of observing religious beliefs and practices.

As regards the information pertaining to their daily prayers, the table given below depicts it.

Table 3.35: Performance of Prayers in a Day Before Widowhood

SI. No.	*Performance of prayers in a day*	*Frequency*	*Percentage*
1	Once a day	206	82.4
2	Twice a day	33	13.2
3	Never	11	4.4
Total		250	100.0

The above table depicts the prayers performed by widows in a day. Majority of the respondents 82.4% (206) are performing prayers once in a day, whereas 13.2% (33) were performing twice in a day and 4.4% (11) of them were not at all performing prayers in a day. Even after widowhood Veerashaiva women continue their religious activities, through which they get some mental satisfaction. But we may find variations in their numbers. Those who stopped performing prayers in a day, they felt that they might again start the performance of prayers after some time.

An attempt is made to record the feelings of widows immediately after the death of their husbands. It is presumed that the initial period is crucial as it creates in them a sense of helplessness and withdrawal from routine life. The widows were asked to narrate their feelings in this regard. A considerable dislocation of routine work was noticed. The daily prayers also were neglected. The table given below depicts the situation. The effects of widowhood on the religious activities were observed.

Table 3.36: The Effect of Widowhood is for (period)

Sl. No.	*Period*	*Frequency*	*Percentage*
1	1 - 3 years	203	81.2
2	4 - 6 years	36	14.4
3	7 years and above	11	4.4
Total		250	100.0

The data presented in the above table reveals that 81.2% (203) widows experienced the grievance of widowhood upto 1-3 years, whereas 14.4% (36) widows experienced the grievance of widowhood upto 4-6 years and 4.4% (11) widows experienced for more than 7 years. It means, they were not at all performing any type of religious activities like, festivals, worshipping the saints, going to temple, *pooja* of *istalinga* and attending religious discourses etc. Thus the effect of any bad event in the life of an individual is for a few years. The integration of widows is a bit difficult task during the first few years of the event. Most of them appeared to be returning to normal life after three years.

One of the religious activities performed by Veerashaiva women outside home is visiting the temples. This is considered as one of the best mechanisms for the integration of widows to their mainstream of life. For Veerashaivas, visit to temple is regarded as one of the routine activities. It is observed that a number of widows compulsorily visit the temple every day before they take their daily food. There may be slight changes in their activities after widowhood but they do not stop entirely performing religious activities both within home and outside home. In this study the data pertaining to one of the outside religious activities is collected by asking a question. How frequently do you visit temples before and after widowhood? Though Veerashaiva widows perform their routine activity of offering prayers to Istalinga at home, their movements outside the home appear to be restricted. The data on their movement outside the home was collected. The analysis of the data is presented in the table given below.

Table 3.37: How Frequently Did You Go to the Temple Before Widowhood?

Sl. No.	*Visit to Temple*	*Frequency*	*Percentage*
1	Daily	34	13.6
2	Once in a week	70	28.0
3	Once in a month	68	27.2
4	On festival days	65	26.0
5	Never	13	5.2
Total		250	100.0

The above table shows that, about 34 widows constituting 13.6 % were visiting temples regularly, 28% (70) of them were visiting temples once a week, 27% (68) were visiting once in a month, 26% (65) were visiting on festival days and 5.2% (13) were not at all visiting temples before their widowhood.

It can be further inferred from the table that majority of (28%) them were visiting once in a week on one fixed day. Whereas (27.2%) widows opined that they were visiting once in a month i.e., on no-moonday (Amavasye) and (26%) were visiting on certain occasions like festival days, and (5.2) were never visiting the temples. A few of them reported that they were so busy in doing the work, they did not get time to visit and a few answered that they did not have a mind to visit temples.

Even after widowhood there is no restriction for performing religious activities both inside and outside the house. This study also intends to collect the information about performing religious activities even after widowhood to find the variations in their activities. Their outside religious activity like visiting the temples after widowhood reveals that most of the widows started visiting the temples to have the blessings for better future for them and their children; it may be owing to the function of religion to provide relief from the stress and strain. The table given below depicts the percentage distribution of Veerashaiva widows visiting temples after their widowhood.

Table 3.38: Respondents Visit to Temples After Widowhood

SI. No.	*Visit to Temple*	*Frequency*	*Percentage*
1	Daily	27	10.8
2	Once in a week	28	11.2
3	Once in a month	60	24.0
4	On festival days	98	39.2
5	Never	37	14.8
Total		250	100.0

The statistical data shows that, the Veerashaiva widows are visiting temples even after their widowhood. There is a slight change in their frequency of visits to temples. It is noticed that 10.8% (27) of them are visiting temples daily, 11.2% (28) are visiting once in a week, 24% (60) are visiting once in a month, 39.2% (98) are visiting on festival days while 48% (37) are not at all visiting temples.

It can be further inferred from the table that on comparing their visit to temple before widowhood, we find that majority (90) of them constituting 36% are visiting temples only on festival days or occasionally due to their depression in life and also due to the responsibility of family. They did not get time to visit the temples more frequently, on the other hand some other widows reported that they began visiting more frequently because they were getting some mental peace.

Another religious activity outside the house of Veerashaiva widows is related to the attending religious discourses like Puranas, Kiratanas, Shastras etc,. The study of 250 widows shows that, this type of activity is mostly found among old widows. The young widows were not inclined to attend them as they were deeply shocked over the crises. They feel for a while disinterested in routine activities. They hesitate to show their faces to the public and do not wish to come into contact with the public. As time goes on and the duration of widowhood increases she adjusts to the life of widowhood and wishes to attend certain religious discourses. Such occasions make her to come into contact with community people. The following table describes the situation.

Table 3.39: Attending Religious Discourses After Widowhood

SI. No.	*Visit to Temple*	*Frequency*	*Percentage*
1	Yes	130	52.0
2	No	120	48.0
Total		250	100.0

The above table shows that, about 52% (130) respondents are attending the religious discourses after their widowhood, while 48% (120) are not attending. It can be further inferred that during their earlier period more than half of them constituting 52% are attending and less than half of them constituting 48% are not attending.

There are many restrictions laid on widows in Hindu and other communities. Restrictions are about wearing the dress and ornaments, eating food, participation in marriage and other religious rituals. However, there are no restrictions on widows in Veerashaiva community so far as the religious rights are concerned. While describing the nature of restrictions laid on widows in Hindu and Veerashaiva communities, Ishwaran has said "... In the Brahmanical culture a widow is regarded as inauspicious and the belief is promoted that an inadvertent sight of her early in the day will ruin one's transactions for the day. The Brahman widow cannot participate in any auspicious rites or ceremonies, and she is strictly prohibited from making her presence visible on such occasions. In total contrast, a Lingayat widow can participate freely in her own right, in marriage ceremonies, worshipping and religious festivities". In this connection, there is a mention found in the *District Gazetteer,* "The Lingayata widow may use a sari of any colour, continue to wear the bodice and may wear ornaments, except the nosering, the lucky neck-thread and toe-rings".

This study tries to know the religious activities performed by widows both inside as well as outside the home. Religious activities inside the home are those performed within home itself like poojas, festivals, worshipping the saints (death anniversaries), and the religious activities outside the home are going to temple, attending religious discourses, attending fairs and festivals.

The veerashaiva women perform both inside as well as outside religious activities. They perform various poojas like Varadashankar pooja, Sampat Shukravar, Mangalagouri, Sola Somavara, Rudrabhisheka, Laxmi pooja, Ambabhavani pooja (Deepa Hakuvadu) etc, and do fast on some pooja days. A Lingayat widow can participate freely in religious festivities. Though she loses her right to the bridal vermilion mark on the forehead and the wedding bracelet of black beads, the Lingayat widow is spared from the further humiliations that are the lot of a widow in the non-populistic Brahmanical culture. Thus in our study the information regarding the religious activities performed by widows just like their earlier life was collected and presented in the table. To collect this information we asked a question, "Are you performing as many religious activities as you were performing before your widowhood?"

Table 3.40: Distribution of Respondents by Their Performance of Religious Activities

Sl. No.	*Response*	*Frequency*	*Percentage*
1	Yes	235	94.0
2	No	15	6.0
Total		250	100.0

The above table depicts that majority 94% (235) of widows are celebrating as many religious activities as they were performing in their earlier days. While very less number of them 6% (15) are not performing all activities. Some of them have stopped certain activities like festivals which fall on the days their husbands have lost their life. It can be further inferred that about 94% of them answered that they could not away from religious practices for long and when children were there observance of festivals and other religious activities became almost compulsory.

This study also intends to know the changes that occur in the life of respondents after they become widowed. Widows are subjected to many restrictions and society also expects a peculiar way of life from them. These restrictions are reflected in their action pattern and ways of life. The death of the husband merely brings changes in the following aspects of widowed life. Changes in wearing dress and ornaments, changes in their economic condition, changes in their contact with the community members, and changes in their status. As far as changes in wearing dress and ornaments are concerned, almost all widows stop using the vermilion. Few young widows are using the bindi (Tikali). Elderly widows stop using the glass bangles. Instead they start using silver bangles, because material culture changes faster than the non-material culture. All widows stop wearing the mangalasutra, while there is no restriction in wearing dress among Veerashaivas, most of the widows stop using costly dresses but again after few years of their widowhood some start wearing costly dresses to maintain the standard of their family. They also stop wearing ornaments which increase the beauty of a woman. Whose economic condition is very poor they start doing one or the other income generating activity for their livelihood. A few others start managing household activities including field activities. While few others change their food habits. Immediately after the death of her husband widow cannot talk freely with other men, especially the young widows, whereas aged widows have little bit freedom. From our study it can be inferred that women cannot go freely outside the home after becoming widows, because community looks at them suspiciously, but the case may differ from widow to widow. The young widows do not participate actively in auspicious occasions like marriage and birth ceremonies. They will watch the ceremonies. But as time passes they start participating in their family ceremonies. Because in Veerashaiva community widows are not regarded as inauspicious. This study intends to notify a very significant point. That is segregation of widows as practised in Brahmins. It is not the case with Veerashaiva widows. They are not deprived of the routine activities to a great extent.

3.7 Widows and Social Participation in Society

Promilla Kapur in her study expresses the view that, "Man exists independently while woman exists in relation to him". She is only recognised as a daughter or a wife, by the society. This social recognition of woman as a dependent person undermines her personal interests, attainments and ambitions. Thus her whole existence is expected to fulfil and complement man's desires, ambitions and prestige. Even the widows have no exception from it. This part of the thesis deals with the social participation of Veerashaiva widows. A widow's social participation implies her life outside the home. Does she exist and participate in the community life, just as she did before widowhood? Is she allowed to participate in recreational activities? How often does she go out to meet friends, relatives, cinema etc? Did she go out more often when her husband was alive? Do any friends give visit to her house? How is she utilizing her leisure time? When did she start to attend the marriage ceremonies after the death of her husband?, The reactions of the respondents towards these questions are being analysed.

The social participations of widows include their relations with their personal friends, neighbours in addition to their family members and husband's friends. Society prescribes a set of norms which have to be strictly adhered to by her, failing which she will be ostracised. These restrictions made her to cut off certain social relations. In order to get an information regarding her outside home activity as a part of social participation, we asked "How often do you go out to meet friends, relatives, etc?"

Table 3.41: Opinion of Respondents About Going Out to Meet Friends, Relatives and to See Cinema etc.

Sl. No.	*Period*	*Frequency*	*Percentage*
1	Daily	2	0.8
2	Once a week	83	33.2
3	Twice a week	11	4.4
4	Once a month	87	34.8
5	Occasionally	16	6.4
6	Never	51	20.4
Total		250	100.0

In large joint families widow's life was confined to the four walls of the house. The possibility of having a personal friends and visits to relatives was limited to the household alone. Sometime they could meet friends, relatives, at public places like, temples, markets, at the common water tap etc., very rarely they could give purposive visit to them. The data presented in the above table deals with the frequency of visits of respondents to friends, relatives, neighbours etc. It can be inferred from the data stated above that majority (34.8%) of respondents are visiting friends, relatives, once in a month while very less number (0.8%) of respondents are visiting daily the nearby friends and relatives, few of (6.4%) them are visiting occasionally when certain functions are being performed in their homes. But it is noticed that (20.4%) respondents are never giving visits to them because of their old age and frequent illness, and some young widows hesitate to show their faces to the community people. When they go out most of the widows accompany their children, parents, friends, relatives etc. Next to children, most of them are accompanied by friends, neighbours. In general, it can be stated that children will fill the vacuum created in the mental, emotional and financial spheres. To this observation one more item could be added as a factor of social participation of Veerashaiva widows before their widowhood. It tries to analyse the respondents being away from home even before their widowhood by asking "Did they go out frequently when their husband was alive?" The field data reveals most of (73.2%) them were not going out more frequently when their husbands were alive, as they reported that the complete responsibility of the family was on the husband and hence she had the limited role of visiting the relatives and friends. While very few of (26.8%) them opined that, they were going out more frequently with their husbands. Now they have stopped being away from home because of the loss of their partners and loss of interest in life.

The social participation of widows can further be understood by the visits of neighbours, relatives and friends to them.

Table 3.42: Do Any Friends, Neighbours, Relatives Visit You?

Sl. No.	Response	Frequency	Percentage
1	Yes	210	84.0
2	No	40	16.0
Total		250	100.0

The above table depicts the visits of friends, neighbours and relatives to widows. About 210 (84%) widows stated that, relatives, friends, neighbours were giving visits to their houses, just as they did before widowhood, and exchanging their joys and sorrows. Such an attitude of neighbours helped them to take courage and face the ordeal of life. Whereas 40 (16%) related their poor conditions and stated that no one cared to visit them and provide any kind of solace to them.

Social participation of widows also includes the attending of the social and religious functions/rituals. The death of the husbands makes them to be deprived. After sometime gradually they feel it inevitable for them to attend those functions. The table given below depicts the situation.

Table 3.43: When Did You Start Attending Social and Religious Functions/Rituals?

Sl. No.	Period	Frequency	Percentage
1	After 1 - 2 years	172	68.8
2	After 3 - 4 years	30	12.0
3	After 5-6 years	6	2.4
4	After 7 - 8 years	5	2.0
5	9 years and above	7	2.8
6	Not yet	30	12.0
Total		250	100.0

The statistical data shows that a maximum (172) number of widows started attending the social and religious functions/rituals after 1-2 years which is a very critical period for them, about 30 widows started attending/participating after 3-4 years, 6 widows started after 7-8 years, 7 widows attended after 9 years while 30 widows did not attend any of the socio-religious functions. The reasons given for not attending social functions are either they felt discriminated against or out of place, the lack of respect and good treatment that is meted out to them and the sense of alienation they experienced at such places. The other reasons are those of old age, ill-health, etc. A few also disclosed disinterest after the death of their husbands in participating in such functions.

They were further probed in the matter by asking a question "Do you feel unhappy because you are not allowed to participate in religious and ritual activities?" It was found out that a majority (60%) of widows felt unhappy because they were not allowed to have active participation in religious and ritualistic activities. The others stated that they did not feel unhappy as they were not personally interested in moving out of the house. The widows were looked upon as inauspicious and therefore could not participate in auspicious festivities such as marriage or other auspicious occasion.

Social participation of widows also includes the leisure time activities of widows. The information pertaining to their leisure time activities both before and after widowhood is essential to understand the co-curricular activities of the respondents as a part of social participation. This study found out that the leisure time activities of the Veerashaiva widows are various. Majority of widows were spending their leisure time in doing one or the other household activities (preparing warm quilts, dairy farming, working in the field etc.). Some of the respondents were spending their leisure time in increasing their existing knowledge (reading, writing and watching T.V. etc.), where as some were doing some handicraft works (tailoring, knitting and embroidery) during their leisure time. Collecting the fuel, doing social service activities and gossiping are the leisure time activities of the widows. It is noticed from this study that for majority of (85.2%) widows change of work i.e., doing one or the other activity is their leisure time activity while very less number (14.8%) of them opined that taking rest is leisure time activity for them before their widowhood.

But after their widowhood, due to the burden of maintaining and running the family and working both inside and outside the family perhaps provides them very little time for themselves. The leisure time activities of widows are similar to those before widowhood with slight changes. An analysis of the leisure time activities of them after their widowhood reveals that preparing home made carpets, dairy farming, working in the field, indulging in watching T.V., listening to radio, indulging in literary activities like reading, writing, taking rest, tailoring, knitting and embroidery, collecting fuel, preparing papads, doing social service activities, meeting friends, coaching the children, performing prayers and attending religious discourses and gossiping are their major leisure time activities.

REFERENCES

1. Talcott Parsons; 1958: *Essays in Sociological Theory,* Revised Edition, Light and Life Publishers, New Delhi, p. 232.
2. Stephan Mennel, 1985: *Students Encyclopedias of sociology,* Macmillan Press Ltd., p. 172.
3. Lopata, H.Z.: *Widowhood in an American City,* Cambridge, MA,
4. Mclaughery, J. (1980): "Neighbourhood revitalization" in P. Drignan and A. Reavushka (ed.) the United States in the 1980s. Stanford, C.A. Hoover Institution Press, p. 16.
5. National Commission on Neighbourhood; 1979: Neighbourhood, People, building Neighbourhoods. With a two Volume appendix Washington Government Printing Office, p. 16.

6. Hunter, A., (1974) : "Symbolic Communities", in *The Persistence of Change in Chicago's Communities,* Chicago, University of Chicago Press, p. 16.
7. Shanas, et al.,: *The Health of Older People: A Social Survey,* Cambridge, Massachusetts, Harvard University Press, 1962.
8. *Ibid.*
9. Hochschild, Arlie Russell: *The Unexpected Community,* Englewood Cliffs, Prentice-Hall.
10. Atchley, R.C.; 1975: "Dimensions of Widowhood in later life", *The Genrontlogist* 15(April): 176-178.
11. Morgan, Leslie A. 1981: "Economic Change at Mid-life widowhood: A Longitudinal Analysis", *Journal of marriage and Family,* Vol. 43(4) p. 899.
12. Corcoran, Mary, 1979: "The Economic consequences of marital dissolution for women in the middle years", *Sex Roles,* 5:343-353. See also, Holden, Karen. C., Richard, V. Burkhauser, and Danid A. Myers. 1986: "Income transitions at older stages of life; The dynamics of poverty," *Gerontologist,* 26:292-297. See also.

    Hyman, Herbert H.: 1983: *Of Time and Widowhood,* Durhman NC Duke University Press. See also.

    Morgan, Leslie A., 1981: "Economic Changes at Mid life Widowhood: A longitudinal analysis", *Journal of Marriage and Family,* 43.899-912. See also.

    Zick, Cathleen D., and Ken, R. Smith; 1986: "Intermediate and delayed effects of widowhood on poverty; patterns from the 1970s", *Gerontologist,* 26:660-75.
13. Lopata, H.Z. 1973: *Widowhood in An American city,* Cambridge: Schenckman Publishing Company.
14. Morgan, L.A. 1979: "Economic impact of widowhood in a pan of middle-aged women", Unpublished dotoral dissertation, University of Southern California.
15. *Op.cit:* p. 900.
16. Bane; 1975.
17. Palmor et al; 1966: *Widows with children under Social security.* Washington.D.C. U.S. Government Printing Office. See also.

Morgan, L.A.; 1976: "A re-examination of widowhood and morale", *Journal of Gerontology* 31 (Nov): 687-695. See also.

Steinhart, F.A.; 1976: "An emprirical test of the Sobol-Hoffman Occupational engagement model", Paper Presented at the Illinois Sociological Association Meetings, Chicago. See also.

Walther, R.J., and L.A. Morgan, 1978: "Work and School; Following Women throgugh Widowhood".

18. Lopata: Living Arrangements of American Urban Widows, *Sociological Focus* 5, 1971, 41-61.

19. Carol R. Ember and Melvin Ember; 1977: *Anthropology,* second Edition Prentice-Hall, Inc, Englewood Cliffs, New Jersey, p. 382.

20. D.N. Majumdar and T.N. Madan: *An Introduction to Social Anthropology;* Asia Publishing House, New York, p. 157.

21. *Ibid.*, p. 157.

22. Rekhadevi Raju; 1988: *Status of Women,* Dastane Ramchandra & Co, 830. Sadashiv Peth, Poona, 30, p. 147.

23. Altekar, A.S.: *The Position of Women in Hindu Civilization.* Motilal Banarsidas, Delhi 1938.

24. Kumar Swamiji: *Mirror of Virashaivism,* pp. 83-84.

25. Poojya Dr. Sharanabasawappa Appa; 1992: President's Speech; 21st All India Veerashaiva Mahasabha, Belgaum, pp. 4.

26. Nandimath, S.C. 1942: *Handbook of Virasaivism,* Dharwar, pp. 169-70.

27. Iswaran (Dr.)K.: p. 13.

28. Government of Maharashtra (Ed): *Kolhapur District Gazetteer,* p. 180.

4

Problems of Integration of Widows in Veerashaiva Community in the Context of Changing Order

An analysis of the position and status of women/widows during Vedic times reveals that they enjoyed a high status. The birth of a girl was not regarded as inauspicious, and marriage was not regarded as compulsory. A girl in Vedic India waited until she could find the right partner for marriage, failing which she could even decide to remain unmarried even she had a sense of security due to her right to paternal property. Child marriages were unknown and divorcees were permitted. Widows were also allowed to remarry if they wished, and they were neither disfigured nor prevented from wearing jewels. According to *Satapatha* IV (1.5.9.) "May these women suffer not the pangs of widowhood". Let these women without shedding any tears and without sorrow first proceed to the house wearing valuable ornaments[1]. Thus we see that widows enjoyed considerable status and authority during Vedic times.

During post-Vedic period the status of women slowly began to decline. As marriage came to be considered as a goal for women, the charity of widow was doubted and hence she came to be looked down upon. A proverbial high caste, young widow is described as one "Who is drudge of all work, in her father-in-law's tears"[2]. Many widows were forced to commit sati and even young virgin widows were sacrificed on the funeral pyre of their husbands. This evil custom of Sati showed that a woman's life was regarded as a burden and she was not allowed any freedom. She was despised and socially boycotted if she failed to commit sati. Fear and sexual exploitation by the other male members of the family or society made her lead a life of misery. She was disfigured and made physically unattractive, kept in isolation and forced to observe a certain strict code of conduct. She was deprived of participating in social and religious rituals. While a widower was encouraged to remarry after the death of his wife, a lot of disabilities were imposed on women who were widowed.

With the advent of the Brithish rule several social-legal changes began to take place. Raja Ram Mohan Roy campaigned against sati and sati was abolished by law. The Widow Remarriage Act of 1856 permitted widows to remarry. Yet the position and status of women/widows did not change much partly because of the reluctance on the part of women to reform themselves and partly due to society itself which perpetuated their low status particularly that of widows who were doubly exploited.

The year 1947 put an end to the British imperialism and gave India her long due independence. The Government of India, under the leadership of Jawaharlal Nehru, had ambitious plans for the country, to make her strong and progressive. The Government also realised the need to initiate a new scheme of legal reforms for Indian women to improve their position in society. With the advent of independence the right to equality of status, equal opportunity in education and public employment was conferred. The preamble to the constitution of India speaks of securing for all citizens of India equal status, opportunity and justice—social, economic and political. Article 14, 15 and 16 of Constitution ensure equality before law, prohibit discrimination and guarantee equality of opportunity to all citizens in matters relating to religion, employment or appointment to any office. It prohibits discrimination on the grounds of religion, race, caste and sex. The directive principles of the constitution also guarantee equality to women, the right to divorce, the right to remarry and the right to property.

Inspite of all this legal freedom guaranteed in the constitution and by the law, the position of women even after 45 years of independence has not changed much. Women continue to suffer indignities and are treated like second class citizens and are subjected to humiliation and ill-treatment in society and this is specially true of widows.

4.1 The Problem of Integration of Widows

While women are constantly being victimised and exploited by society, widows are the victims of double exploitation by virtue of their being single. They lack the protection of a man and sometimes of a family and therefore they are exploited economically, socially, psychologically and sexually. With industrialisation and urbanisation the socio-economic parameters of the Indian society have changed rapidly. This has led to the break up of the joint family which was a sort of insurance against all calamities. The widows who once had a sort of social security in such families are now exposed to economic distress and social exploitation. Economically they find it very difficult to make both ends meet single handed. The problem of bringing up of children and of providing for their education and marriage becomes the primary goal of their lives. The position of widows who are economically dependent is worse. They are harassed by their own family members and relatives. This constant feeling of dependence often makes them miserable. In a male dominated society widows find it extremely difficult to live. Socially victimised and psychologically depressed widows play the dual role of both men and women and in the process face a lot of problems. 'Despite the protection accorded to them by the Widow Remarriage Act of 1929 and the Hindu Marriage Act of 1954, there has been little change in the basic status of widows'[3]. Eventhough many constitutional problems of widows may differ from community to community, eventhough Rajaram Mohan Roy struggled for the abolition of child marriage, the stress and strain of widows are continuing. Due to many changes in economic order and joint family the problems of widows of any community will be same at least the first ten years.

The problems that the widows face may be classified broadly as economic, social, health and emotional. They are interrelated and the degree of their seriousness varies with the widow's age, economic condition, family structure, religious norms etc.

4.2 Economic Problems

Woman in India is even today dependent, whether she works in the house, in the farm or in any other place. It is the man who is the head of the family and the person in charge of the family transactions. All the monetary transactions are made in his name and he is the owner of the property. When such a person dies his wife finds it hard to adjust to the changed conditions. Whether the widow belongs to rich, middle or poor family, she has in one way or the other problems connected with finance along with other matters.

Most of the widows reported a variety of large number of widows experienced financial difficulties in meeting the basic needs of children such as providing good food, clothing and school fees, maintaining their previous standard of living, paying back loans taken by the husband, etc. Meeting the wedding expenses of children and the provision of dowry to daughters were indicated by a considerable number of respondents. Because when her husband dies the income of the family naturally decreases. Now she has to depend upon herself. At times she is not used to working outside but has to make efforts to find herself a job and become more active in her day today living. Sometimes, she has to work reluctantly as she finds no other way of making both ends meet. A little help in the form of money or kind might come from her parents, sons, brothers, sisters, maternal uncles, in-laws and other relatives, friends and neighbours but this help may not be either adequate or be a constant source to depend upon. A high proportion of the widows experienced income inadequacy to meet their routine needs[4]. The problems of widow become worse if she has many children. At times, she sends her children to do manual type of work to supplement her earnings. In one study, it was reported that fifty percent of the widows were able to maintain their previous standard of living, but only 25 percent were living comfortably and were reasonably free from financial worries[5]. Most frequently items on which they tried to cut down the expenses were clothing, food, social and recreational activities.

The widows belonging to the middle and rich classes also face financial difficulties particularly when they are uneducated and ignorant. Research studies have shown that a few aged widows in the rich as well as in the poor families enjoyed a high status.

4.3 Problems Related to Personal and Social Life

A widow gets emotionally disturbed by sudden shock she receives from the death of her husband. She loses interest in her daily life; and neglects her health which in turn has its repercussion upon her health. Lack of social contact, sense of loneliness and other factors affect her health adversely. Peter Marris says, "In the first place, many had suffered from physical symptoms which, in their own opinion, or that of their doctor, were caused or aggravated by the shock of their husbands' death-loss of weight; rheumatism and filorositis, asthama, bronchitis and cramping pains in the chest; recurrence of duodenal ulcers, gastric ulcers, indigestion; swollen feet and ulcers of the legs; falling hair, aches, dizziness and nervousness"[6]. Some of their health problems are commonly associated with severe emotional conflict. She becomes restless, agitated and creates a tense situation for herself and for others. She becomes irritated and frustrated because of her distressed mind. She becomes apathetic and overwhelmed with a sense of emptiness of life. She may show signs of withdrawal from friends and relatives and loses all interest in her life. It is particularly true with those widows who are young and childless for first few years of their widowhood. A great majority of the widows quoted that they found it difficult to entertain male visitors in the house and felt the lack of a male escort for social functions. They also emphasised that they lacked companionship. Tendency on the part of the widows to withdraw from others and reject consolation has been reported by the author.

Similar observations were also made by Lopata who reported that most of the widows felt lonely. They stated that they missed the partner, felt the lack of some one to care for, experienced a drop in status and expressed an inability to make new friends[7].

The widow is socially incapacitated. The apathy and withdrawal tend to isolate the widow from social life. As it is already known that widow in every community is forbidden to wear Tali, apply Kumkum, wear flowers and participate in all those activities which are considered ritualistically important. Though some old widows may be approached for, advice and guidance and participation in 'Suragi Niru' among few subcastes of Veerashaivas but most of them are not allowed to create pollution. They are regarded as inauspicious and supposed to lead a gloomy and lonely life of enforced celibacy in the society.

Though widow's remarriage is legalised it does not

carry the same sanctity and sacredness as that of her first marriage. The second marriage which is called "Udaki" marriage in some parts of the Karnataka State, is more prevalent in the low caste groups. This marriage brings a mate to the woman, and the children born of this alliance have legal sanctity. But the woman is not received by the people to participate in ritualistic activities. However, this traditionally maintained institutional arrangement has been a source of help to the widow and her children, and a device to mitigate her miseries.

The various problems of widows discussed above may be understood statistically by the table given below.

Table 4.1: Distribution of Respondents by Their Problems After the Death of their Husband

Sl. No.	*Problems of Widows*	*Frequency*	*Percentage*
1	Food	108	43.2
2	Shelter	108	43.2
3	Clothing	122	48.8
4	Education	166	66.4
5	Marriage of children	106	42.4
6	Financial problem	143	57.2
7	Child rearing	104	41.6
8	Loss of marital status	199	79.6
9	Lack of companionship	218	87.2
10	Presence not welcomed at auspicious functions	159	63.6
11	Facing criticism from daughters-in-law	7	2.8

Respondents were made to reveal wherein they felt handicapped due to the absence of the head of the household. This can be understood by the information presented in the above table. About 43.2% of widows complained of food as their major problem, 43.2% are facing shelter problem, 48.8% are facing clothing problem, 66.4% are facing the problem of educating the children, 42.4% widows faced the problem of child rearing, 79.6% worried for the loss of marital status, 87.2% worried for the lack of companionship, 63.6% worried, because their presence is not welcomed in the auspicious function, 2.8% are facing the criticisms from their daughters-in-law.

It can be further inferred from the table that, a high proportion of widows felt the financial stress of maintaining the family by themselves without the support of other family members. They are also facing problems centred around taking decisions about the education, occupation and marriage of their children. A majority of the non-working widows, being of an older age group, reported ill-health, old age, loneliness and lack of mental stability as their personal problems. A few other respondents reported that, bringing up small children, marriage and education of children seem to be the major problems. Other averred that they were degraded and made to feel inferior because of their single status.

Ill-treatment and indifferent treatment and differences of opinion with married sons and their spouses seemed to be the major problems faced by the widows. They complained of daughters-in-law not making necessary adjustments and there by facing many criticisms from them and creating misunderstanding in the family. Often the daughters-in-law did not want them to stay in the house. The constant friction in the family and the unhappy environment caused them to feel lonely.

In general the majority of the widows feel lonely, insecure, deserted or frustrated. The fact that people suffering from a conjugal bereavement also suffer from an elevated risk of physical deterioration and death offers testimony to the stressful nature of such a loss (Jacobs and Ostfelf 1977; Rees and Luttkar 1967). It may be concluded that a considerable proportion of the widows faced problems of money. Child-rearing, personal and social life. Lack of companionship, loss of marital status, were the major problems indicated by the Veerashaiva widows of Gulbarga.

Gurmeet, M.P. Singh and Sukhdeep Gill in their study, highlighted that the widows faced problems of money, child-rearing and personal and social life, taking care of children, purchasing items of luxury, maintaining "give and take" with friends and a lack of companionship. Even in our study also the major problems indicated by widows are somewhat similar to them.

Peter Marris (1958:10) in his study of "Widows and their Families" says when her husband dies the widow has to adjust to her new state while she is preoccupied with a painful struggle to master her grief. For months even after his death, her energies may be so absorbed in this struggle, and her feelings so deeply distributed, as to affect all her needs and her response to those who try to meet them. The problems of widows are normally related to their condition of deprivation, alienation and oppression. As widows, they are deprived of psychological, social and economic securities associated with their relationship to the husband. Unfortunately, widows are conserved as bad women and hence are doubly deprived and oppressed. The already exploited and deprived women will be subjected to further deprivation as widows. Hence for an adequate analysis of the problem, the study of integration of widows in the context of changing order is essential.

In India, the social structure is constituted of classes defined in relation to their role in social production against the background of caste. Caste accentuates class exploitation through mythical and religious (ritual) legitimation. Women, besides being subjected to such exploitation, are further deprived of and oppressed on the basis of gender discrimination and widowhood leads to further loss of status resulting in an alarming state of helplessness and hopelessness[8].

Family is the basic unit which provides protection to the human beings. Even after the death of the husband the woman has to live within the family. It is said that a house is everything to a woman. With the death of the bread-winner her role undergoes a total change. If she is young or middle aged, she has to live with the support of her relatives along with her children. The elderly widows live with their sons. They cannot have a separate establishment after their widowhood. As the widow is socially incapacitated, she is to lead a gloomy and lonely life of enforced celibacy in the society. In the words of Cormack (1953:174)[9] a widow "in her parents' house is a burden and is treated as a servant. She gets sympathy, but not much and she is often considered the cause of her husband's death". With all these griefs she has to integrate herself within the society.

Today Indian woman is marching forward, to be free from age, old barriers of slavery and mental tyranny. She is working in all fields like schools, colleges, universities, offices, hospitals alike. We have today, woman air-pilot, woman mountaineer, woman aeronaut, woman executive, woman soldier, woman engineer, woman lawyer, woman Vice-chancellor. The changing order has facilitated her to be free from mental tyranny. It has been replaced by a new era with freedom as her birthright, education as her privilege. With Hindu Marriage Act, Succession Act, widow Remarriage Act, Sharada Act, Adoption Act, Prohibition of Dowry Act, Abolition of sati Act and right to maintenance, she has leaped into rivalry with men and emerged successfully as a respectable member of the household. To those who belong to an older generation, merely frown and feel a bit sad when they look their daughters and daughters-in-law shattering or renouncing the values they had so lovingly cherished and carefully safeguarded.

Modernization, urbanization, Industrialization brought changes in the occupational structure of Veerashaiva community Especially the modern facilities and Educational opportunities to women brought changes in their way of life. Even the attitudes of society towards women and especially towards widows are changing. It will be helpful for the integration of widows. This study tried to understand the integration of widows within the Veerashaiva community in the context of changing order. Changing order is nothing but a change in the way of life through modernization, industrialization, employment opportunities for women, educational opportunities, change in occupational structure etc. In order to understand the integration of widows in the context of changing order we collected information by questioning the respondents about the attitude of society towards widows, reactions of widows now and then, whether the modern changes facilitated or not in respect of moving out of widows, Education, decision making, meeting the relatives and friends.

REFERENCES

1. Quoted from Satapatha IV 1.5.9. Gupta, Padmini Sen;1974: *The Story of Women of India,* India Book House, New Delhi, pp. 57.
2. Mehta, Sushila; 1982: *Revolution and Status of women in India,* Metropolitan Books Ltd. pp. 130.
3. Lopamudra: *The Plight of Widows; Social Welfare,* Vol. 29, No. 11-12, p. 13.
4. Lopata; 1973: *Widowhood in American City,* Cambridge: Schenc Kumar Publishing Co.
5. Nucklos; 1973: Widows Study Abstracted in the Journal Supplement Abstract services, *Catalogue of selected Documents in Psychology,* Vol. 3, p. 5.
6. Peter Marris; 1958: *Widows and Their Families,* London Routledge and Kegan Publishers.
7. Lopata; 1979: *Women as Widows- Support System,* New York: Elsevier Publication, p. 89.
8. *Op.cit.,* 10
9. Cormack; 1953: *The Hindu Women,* New York, Columbia University, p. 174.

5

A Review of Social Legislation Pertaining to Widows' Rights and Responsibilities

For the proper assessment of the social and legal position of women, a brief review of the background of Indian women through the ages is essential. In the vedic age, women enjoyed relatively high position in Indian society. They enjoyed freedom for spiritual progress and intellectual development. Vedic texts are replete with references to rituals recommended for ensuring the birth of a learned daughter[1]. During Vedic period women were married at mature age and had full freedom in the choice of their husbands. But during the smruti period the position deteriorated when the injunctions of Manu which codified Hindu life obliterated the practice of Upanayana for women. Manu propounded the theory of perpetual tutelage of women[2].

During the periods of Islam and Mughal rule, the position of women slumped. It touched the lowest ebb during the British period. It was during 19th century, the serious efforts were made by social reformers for giving an honourable position to women within the society.

There were leaders in the 19th century who started social reform movement. Raja Rammohan Roy was one of the first protagonists of women-cause who carried a vigorous campaign against Sati which was ultimately legally prohibited in 1829. Other social reformers viz., D.N. Tagore, Ishwarchandra Vidyasagar, Swami Dayanand Saraswati, fought for the welfare of the women. With the efforts of them today we notice the introduction of female education, remarriage of Hindu widows, prevention of child marriage and removal of polygamy. The efforts of K.C. Sen against early marriages facilitated the enactment of civil marriage Act of 1872. Other social reformers of the 19th Century M.G. Ranade, D.K. Karve, Rabindranath Tagore and others tried to inculcate in women the spirit and values of the society. Even some of the outstanding women of the nineteenth century fought for the welfare of the women. Pandita Ramabai, Ramabai Ranade, Anandibai Joshi and others struggled for raising the social position of women.

The national movement under the leadership of Mahatma Gandhi provided further necessary impetus towards restoration of position of women in Indian society. Gandhiji in his writing in *Young India* (1918) said, "Woman is the companion of man, gifted with equal mental capacities, she has the right to participate in the minutest details of the activities of man and she has the same right of freedom and liberty as he... By sheer force of a vicious custom, even the most ignorant and worthless men have been enjoying a superiority over women which they do not deserve and ought not to have"[3]. With the inspiration from Gandhi's vision of freedom and equality for women and inception of a movement was heralded in the early decade of the twentieth century and it was intended to bring out the welfare of women. Some of the outstanding women leaders of the 20th Century like Sarojini Naidu, Raj Kumari Amrit Kaur, Kamaladevi Chattopadhyaya, Durgabai Deshmukh, Dhanavanti Rama

Rau and many others struggled against the prevalent conditions and pursued with all sincerity the object of women's emancipation.

The spirit in which Mahatma Gandhiji had involved women in the struggle for freedom, has now come to be firmly enshrined in the constitution of Independent India, It promises to secure to all its citizens, "Justice--social, economic and political liberty of thought, expression, belief, faith and worship, equality of status and opportunity, and to promote among them all fraternity, assuring the dignity of the individual and the unity of the Nation"[4]. To attain these objectives the constitution guarantees certain fundamental rights. Indian women are the beneficiaries of these rights in the same manner as Indian men. Article 14 ensures "equality before the law" and Article 15 prohibits "any discrimination", Art. 16(1) guarantees "equality of opportunity for all citizens in matters relating to employment or appointment to any office under the state". Articles that protect and cover the equality of women by implication. There are several other Articles that protect and cover the equality of women by implication. These are: Art. 39(b) (c) (f) (relating to ownership of material resources); Art. 40 (organization of panchayats for self-government); Art. 41 (right to work, employment and public assistance); Art. 43 (provision of work, a living wage etc.); Art. 44 a (uniform civil code); Art. 45 (free and compulsory education for all children upto the age of 14) and Art. 47 (raising the standard of nutrition, standard of living and public health).

Moreover, there are some Articles that have been described by commentators in the Indian constitution as "women-specific" These are: Art. 16 (2) which forbids discrimination in respect to any employment of office under the state "on the grounds only of religion, race, caste, sex, descent, place of birth, residence or any one of them", Art. 39(d) "Equal pay for equal work for both men and women", Art. 39(e) "protection of the health and strength of workers -- men, women and children from abuse and entry into avocations unsuited to their age and strength", Art. 42 "just and humane conditions of work and maternity relief", Art. 325 which says that "no special electoral rules can be made on the grounds of religion, race, caste and sex", and above all Art. 15 (3) which in fact provides for affirmative action and for protective discrimination by empowering the state, to make "any special provision for women and children."

All these constitutional provisions are supported by various legislations. Many of these legislations were initially instituted in, response to the reform movement of the nineteenth century. The Hindu Marriage Act, 1955, the Hindu Succession Act, 1956, the Hindu Minority and Guardianship Act, 1956, the Prohibition of Dowry Act, 1956, were the major steps towards the liberation of women. Several studies conducted recently brought out the fact that women are not enjoying these rights and suffer from a number of socially inexorable disabilities and inhibitions. The social norms and values which govern human behaviour do not favour women suing their rights and thus create obstacles towards the enforcement of legislations which aim at improving the status of women.

The present investigation, which is exploratory in nature and has been carried out in Gulbarga city aims at examining the level of awareness of women of the legal rights which have been made available for them and especially for widows. Other objectives of the present investigation include examination of the awareness of legislation pertaining to property inheritance, providing job of their husband to them after their death, law pertaining to death registration, legislation pertaining to share given in father's property, awareness regarding providing widow pension, attitude of widows towards widow remarriage, recommending restrictions put forth on widows, providing employment opportunities for widows, etc., in the context of changing status of women.

A number of studies on awareness of legal rights have

been conducted. Some of the important studies are of Fairchild (1961), Government of India (1974), Mathur (1977, Kaur and Sharma (1983), Sachchidananda (1984), Mishra (1986) and Minattus (1977). These studies cover both rural and urban women. All these studies show that the level of awareness of women is very poor. Awareness is found to be high among the urban working women. The least awareness prevails among the illiterate rural women.

In this study, the focus is only on widows. We tried to know their awareness regarding different aspects of women's life protected by different legislations in the country. It has been assumed that there is a positive relationship between the level of education and that of awareness of legal rights. With the increase in the educational level of the persons, the level of their awareness increases. The degree of awareness of each of the aforementioned laws was assessed by asking the respondents if they ever heard of each of the legal possession. The overall response was taken for examining awareness of legal rights. Awareness in the present case is being defined as knowledge among women either general or specific awareness is devoid of knowledge of provisions of legal rights, i.e., women/widows simply know and have heard that rights are there and specific or complete awareness, one in which women know and enumerate either partially or fully the major provision of the legal rights available to them.

As it has already, been mentioned, legal rights, viz., Inheritance (property right), law pertaining to providing job of their husbands to them, law pertaining to death registration, share given in father's property, awareness regarding widow remarriage act of 1856, law pertaining to widow pension, are in vogue since Independence. But these rights seem to have yet to permeate the Hyderabad Karnataka region as the bulk of the respondents appear to be absolutely ignorant of their legal rights.

In this part of the thesis an attempt is being made to enumerate the widows' awareness of legal rights.

5.1 Awareness of Property Rights

The Hindu Succession Act, 1956 has relaxed the property laws for women/widows, Hindu women from the time of ancient law givers, were debarred from possessing property in their own right. A woman could only own her stridhana or bridal ornaments, etc., which were settled on her at the time of her marriage. The *Dayabhag* system allowed sons to have an equal share in the father's property in Bengal, but a daughter had no right of inheritance. The *Mitakshara,* on joint family system, also allowed no share to the women. Thus, economically handicapped women naturally remained subordinate to men right through the British period, though the Hindu women's Right to Property Act was passed in 1937, allowing a wife to benefit with her husband's share in coparcenary property during her life time. The Hindu Succession Act allows the widow and the mother to inherit the property of the deceased. Each takes an equal share except in the case of coparcenary property, when the son takes his own share plus a share of his father's property. With this Act, women can hold their property, and have the right to sell, mortgage, or give away their property, if they so wish.

The following were the decisive changes brought about by the Act, according to which

1 The Act abolished the Dayabhaga and the Mitakshara School of Hindu law relating to succession.

2 The Act has repealed provisions of different Acts relating to succession under Matriarchal system (prevailing in the south)

3 The Act has abolished Hindu woman's limited estate, and made her absolute owner of the property, even with regard to existing properties.

4 The Act has provided uniform order of succession governing the property of a male Hindu, with a

few changes in respect of the *marumakattayam* and *aliyas-antana* law.

5 The Act has abolished impartible estate, not created by statute.

6 The Act has provided uniform order of succession governing the property of a female Hindu, with a few changes in respect of the *marumakattayam* and *aliyasantana* law.

7 The order of succession provided by the Act is based according to the standard of love and affection, and the rule of preference based on the right to offer *pinda* (followed by the *Dayabhaga*) or propinquity of blood (followed by the *Mitakshara*) has been discarded by the Act.

8 The Act provides simple rules of preference, and where no preference can be made, heirs take simultaneously.

9 The Act entitles, even remotest agnate or cognate to be the heir.

10 The Act makes no distinction between male and female heirs.

11 The Act has given right to certain female heirs, to succeed to the interest of the deceased in the coparcenary property.

12 Disease defect or deformity is no ground of exclusion from inheritance under the Act.

13 The Act entitles a male to dispose off his interest in a Mitakshara coparcenary property by a will.

The Act eliminates the foundations on which the joint family was based by declaring that birth in the family does not give right to property. It also makes woman/ widow an absolute owner of the property and not a limited owner. By this measure, it has placed woman on equal footing with man with regard to the right of use of the property. The Act has also brought about a radical change with regard to the heirs for succession in class. The position of heirs in call I includes, son, daughter, widow, mother, son of a pre-deceased son, daughter of a predeceased son, son of predeceased daughter, daughter of a predeceased daughter, widow of a predeceased son.

The below given table depicts the awareness of respondents regarding the inheritance of property.

Table 5.1: Are You Aware of the Legislation Pertaining to Property Inheritance?

SI. No.	*Response*	*Frequency*	*Percentage*
1	Yes	221	88.4
2	No	29	11.6
Total		250	100.0

As regards awareness of respondents of inheritance of property, bulk of the respondents are aware of the legislation pertaining to property inheritance while very less number of them are unaware of it. It is further interpreted from the table that about 88.4% respondents are more aware and conscious of their rights and duties, whereas very less number, consisting of 11.6% of the respondents who are illiterate are ignorant of the inheritance rules. Those who have shown awareness of inheritance have come mostly from upper age group and these who are illiterates have heard of inheritance.

The right to make a will for his property has been given to the owner of the property. This is a grave flaw in the Act. With the right to will away the property; the owners may circumvent the necessity of devoting the property to daughters and other female members. In this regard we asked a question to respondents; Have you made any will of the property for any body?

Table 5.2: Have You Made Any Will of the Property for Anybody?

Sl. No.	*Response*	*Frequency*	*Percentage*
1	Yes	6	2.4
2	No	244	97.6
Total		250	100.0

The above table depicts whether the respondents have made any will for the inheritance of their property. The table states that a very less number (6) of widows made the will of the property for charity purposes and bulk (244) of them have not made any will of the property. The reasons for this may be the indecision of the owners of property. Sometimes they preferred maintenance of status quo. Hindu Women's Right to Property Act (1973) conferred the right to enjoy her husband's share in coparcenary property for life time without a right to alienate property. Under this Act the daughters, the widows and the mothers can inherit the property of the deceased simultaneously. As between them each takes an equal share, except that where there are more widows than one, all the widows together take one share. This is the position with respect to the self-acquired property of the deceased. With respect to coparcenary property, the son takes his own share in such property and in addition takes a share in the father's share of such property as well, unless he had separated himself from the coparcenary during the life time of his father. Nevertheless, the acceptance of the right of the daughter to inherit is itself a big step forward. Under this Act women/widows will now hold their property absolutely with full right to sell.

Some special provisions have been made regarding the rights of daughters in the family dwelling house or family business. In a dwelling house wholly occupied by members of the family, a female heir, although she may be entitled to live there, cannot ask for her share until and unless the male heirs choose to divide it. Where a female heir inherits an interest in any immovable property or business, if any heir wishes to sell out his or her interest, the other heirs will have a right to purchase. In this regard we asked a question to the respondents: Are you aware of the law that is about share given in father's property?

Table 5.3: Awareness of Share Given in Father's Property

SI. No.	*Response*	*Frequency*	*Percentage*
1	Yes	145	58.0
2	No	105	42.0
Total		250	100.0

The above table depicts the awareness of respondents about the share given in father's property. As regards awareness of respondents, about 145 (58%) are aware of the share given in father's property and 105 (42%) are ignorant about the law. It can be further inferred from the table that more than half of the respondents are aware by hearing and reading, whereas less than half are ignorant about it due to their illiteracy.

5.2 Awareness of Widow Remarriage Act of 1856

The widow Remarriage Act XV, which validated the marriage of widows, was passed in 1856 with the zealous cooperation of Ishwar Chandra Vidyasagar. It also demanded "All rights and interests which any widow may have in her deceased husband's property by way of maintenance, or by inheritance to her husband or to his lineal successors or by virtue of any will or testamentary disposition conferring upon her, without express permission to remarry, only a limited interest in such property with no power of alienating the same, shall upon her remarriage cease and determine as if she had then died and the next heirs of her deceased husband or other persons entitled to the property on her death shall thereupon succeed to the same". The guardianship of the children should dwell upon the male relative of the deceased. The table given below depicts the respondent's awareness regarding the Widow Remarriage Act of 1856.

Table 5.4: Awareness of the Widow Remarriage Act of 1856

Sl. No.	*Response*	*Frequency*	*Percentage*
1	Yes	114	45.6
2	No	136	54.4
Total		250	100.0

It can be inferred from the table that about 114 (45.6%) respondents of Gulbarga city are aware of the widow Remarriage Act of 1856, whereas 136 (54.4%) respondents are shown ignorance. It can be further inferred that 114 widows have only general awareness rather than specific awareness.

5.3 Awareness of the Assistance Given by the Government as Widow Pension

Government is providing a financial assistance to those widows who do not have security from any sources. To find the awareness regarding this we asked a question: Are you aware of the assistance given by the Government as widow pension?

Table 5.5: Awareness of the Assistance Given by the Government as Widow Pension

Sl. No.	*Response*	*Frequency*	*Percentage*
1	Yes	222	88.8
2	No	28	11.2
Total		250	100.0

The above table depicts the percentage distribution of widows by their awareness regarding the assistance given by the Govt., as widow pension. As regards awareness of respondents, about 222 widows are aware of the law, while 28 widows are ignorant about it.

The widows whose husbands were in government services stated that they were aware of the provision of being provided a job in the place of their deceased husbands.

5.4 Awareness of Law Pertaining to Death Registration

The Govt., made a law that every body should register his/her name with the registrar of births and death enumeration. If death occurs in a family it must be registered. It is only that the inheritance of property is possible. One has to get the succession certificate. The table given below depicts the percentage distribution of widows by their awareness regarding the death registration.

Table 5.6: Awareness of Law Pertaining to Death Registration

SI. No.	Response	Frequency	Percentage
1	Yes	108	43.2
2	No	142	56.8
Total		250	100.0

The statistical data presented in the above table shows that about 108 (43.2%) respondents are aware of the death registration law and 142(56.8%) are ignorant about it. It can be further inferred from the table that larger number of widows constituting 56.8% are unaware of the law because of their ignorance. And about 53.2% are aware of the law by hearing or by reading.

As regards awareness of respondents of legal rights education plays an important role in keeping persons abreast with the developments and those who are more educated will be more aware and conscious of their rights and duties. Education dispels ignorance. This turns out to be true in the context of awareness of rights. Those women/widows who are more educated are more aware of their legal rights. Even the occupation of the respondents plays an important role in keeping persons aware of the legal rights. Women/widows with higher level of education, with high media exposure and modernization as well as those who are in employment are more aware of the legal rights than the other.

The laws discussed above have been intended to bring out legal status of women/widows in equality with men. Many widows of the Gulbarga city are quite ignorant of the laws and not much trouble is taken by the authorities to make people aware of them. In order to remove the social inequality in the field of legal provision, it is necessary that laws are implemented adequately and people are educated to follow them.

However a review of different acts passed by different governments from time to time, reveals that some of the problems of women appear to have been partially solved. The Widow Remarriage Act became a boon for the sufferers. Though it has got some serious flaws, the very permission itself has paved the way for the uplift of women. Further, it strengthened the principle of equality, viz., that if a man had the right to remarry, the woman should not be debarred from that privilege.

In the section that follows, we are not making an endeavour to examine widows' opinions and suggestions towards, providing educational facilities towards rehabilitation of widows, provision for widow remarriage removal of restrictions put forth on widows, providing employment opportunities for widows.

Suggestion toward providing educational facilities to the widows needs to be given full consideration. Irrespective of their status they are unanimous on the point of providing education to women.

The respondents' suggestion towards widow remarriage is undertaken for study to analyse the attitude of widows towards remarriage. The table given below depicts the percentage distribution of widows by their attitude towards remarriage.

Table 5.7

Distribution of Respondents by their Recommendation for Provision for Widow Remarriage

SI. No.	*Provision for Widow Remarriage*	*Frequency*	*Percentage*
1	Yes	137	54.8
2	No	62	24.8
3	If she is very young	10	4.0
4	If she has no children	41	16.4
Total		250	100.0

It can be inferred from the above table that about 137(54.8%) respondents suggested provision for widow remarriage, about 62(24.8%) respondents have not suggested the remarriage of widows, while 10(4%) respondents suggested remarriage for those who are very young and 41(16.4%) respondents favoured remarriage for those who have no children.

It can be further inferred from the table that about 54.8% respondents favoured the widow remarriage because the widows will be insecured and suffer from stress and strain. In order to be free from all sorts of problems the remarriage of the widows is a suitable measure for their integration. But 4% respondents suggested that the remarriage of widows must be done only by those who are very young because they donot have a support from anybody and 16.4% respondents suggested remarriage for those who have no children; Leading a lonely life is very difficult, hence the widows should remarry. But 24.8% respondents have unfavourable attitude towards remarriage because the position of remarried women is lower than that of the widows. They were not welcomed on any auspicious functions, but sometimes widows are welcomed as Bhoomitais.

The suggestions of widows towards removal of restrictions put forth on them are noted. Their suggestions have been tabulated. The table given below depicts the situation.

Table 5.8: Do You Suggest Removal of Restrictions Put forth on Widows?

Sl. No.	*Response*	*Frequency*	*Percentage*
1	Yes	225	90.0
2	No	25	10.0
Total		250	100.0

The statistical information presented in the above table shows that majority (90%) of respondents stated that the restrictions on widows should be removed on wearing of dresses, ornaments, attending the auspicious functions, etc., whereas only less number (10%) of respondents i.e. 25 did not suggest removing restrictions, to maintain their position within the society.

The suggestion of widows for providing employment opportunity seems to be genuine, worth taking note of. The government should come forward to create opportunities for them to earn their daily bread.

The preceding analyses, thus, reveal that widows favour all provisions. Favourable attitude has been found more among educated widows rather than among traditional minded ones.

Thus social legislation had also become necessary to meet some of the disabilities and needs of the widows. The government of India has therefore passed some Acts in this direction. The Hindu Marriage Act, 1955, The Hindu Succession Act 1956; and The Hindu Adoption and Maintenance Act, 1956, which include provisions for widow remarriage, succession of property, maintenance, adoption and so on. But it is unfortunate that these legislative measures have not brought many changes, particularly the desired ones, in the status of women in general and that of widows in particular. The reasons may lie in the half-hearted implementation of the Acts and lack of social consciousness among the people.

Needless to say that these statutory provisions have enabled the widows to be socially awakened and economically independent. However, inspite of all these efforts on the part of government and the voluntary organizations the widow still encounters difficulties due to many adverse social and psychological conditions.

REFERENCES

1. *Brihadaranyaka Upanishad,* IV, 4.18, quoted by Asthana, P., *Women's Movement in India,* Vikas, Delhi, p. 1.
2. Shastri, S.R. 1960: *Women in the Vedic age,* Bombay, p. 20.
3. Quoted by Chitnis, S.: A review of the progress made in India towards achievement of the objectives of the international women's decade, Tata Institute of Social Sciences, Bombay, p. 9.
4. *Ibid.*

6

Conclusion

The purpose of the present study is to understand the integration of Veerashaiva widows within family, neighbourhood and community at large in urban setting. In this study an attempt is made to look into the problems faced by widows, the ways they manage these problems and their problems of adjustment. Fieldwork technique is employed to collect the data on integration of widows. Throughout this research exercise, an attempt has been made to explain how widows integrate themselves in all walks of life eventhough they are considered as a second class members of the society. It is our endeavour'-to examine the impact of widowhood on the social living of the Veerashaiva widows of Gulbarga. The impact of widowhood on social, economic and religions aspects of living of widows is highlighted in this study.

The findings are supportive to elicit the problem of integration of widows. Because widowhood is an event that constitutes the greatest and saddest change in the life of a woman. Death of husband brings numerous problems for the widows. In this connection how widows come out from these problems forms one of the major areas of sociological research. Generally it is presumed that the death of the husband brings out changes in the attitude, behaviour and life style of widows. In this connection an effort is made to examine the role of family members, Kith and Kin and neighbours in changing the social life of widows.

Each chapter depicts systematically the problems of integration of widows. Starting from the integration of widows within family and neighbourhood an attempt is made to pin-point the problem in integration by size of family, type of family, and interpersonal relations within the family. The present study tries to understand the problem of integration of widows through their present settlement and type of relationship with their husbands and process of integration, type of support and process of integration, widows and their in-laws, widows parents relations, role of widows within family. The investigation reveals that the widow comes to normal life adjusting to present life and her proper integration within the family takes a considerable time. Maximum number of widows are staying in joint families which appears to be a healthy sign of integration of widows. As the size of the family is large, the widows come in contact with large number of people who help them to be free from the feeling of loneliness.

With regard to widows and in-laws relations, most of the widows have undergone the stiffness of their in-laws which became an obstacle for few days for proper integration of widows within the family. As far as the integration of widows within the neighbourhood is concerned, they maintained their relations just like before widowhood and the constant contact with the neighbours helped them for integration.

It is found that the economic participation of widows within the family helped them for their better integration. In joint family the widows spent their more labour for family and their self sufficiency helped for better economic participation. Most of the widows start working outside the home in order to gain something for livelihood. Those who are economically independent face less stress and strain. The non-working widows, depend completely on other earning members of the family and they do not have any say in economic affairs.

The religious activities are very significant for an individual as they facilitate in maintaining his identity in the community. Whether man, woman or a widow all participate in religious activities. The Veerashaiva widows worship Istalinga regularly, since they do not observe pollution in their menstruation period. Because they believe that Linga has a power of purification of the body. There is nothing like pure or impure for Lingayats. This facilitated them for a better integration. Veerashaivas do not distinguish between man and woman in religious matters. They regard woman as having equal religious status. They do not put restrictions on the performance of religious rituals even after their widowhood, through which they will get some mental satisfaction. But we may find variations in their numbers. Those who stop performing religious rituals, might again start them after some time. Because the initial period is crucial as it creates in them a sense of helplessness and withdrawal from routine life. The integration of widows is a bit difficult task during the first few years of the event. A Lingayat widow can participate freely in religious festivities, though she loses her right to the bridal vermilion mark on the forehead and the wedding bracelet of black beads.

This study also intends to know the changes that occur in the life of respondents after they become widowed. Widows are subjected to many restrictions and society also expects more restrained way of life from them. These restrictions are reflected in their action, pattern and ways of life. The death of the husband brings changes in the following aspects of widowed life—changes in wearing dress and ornaments, changes in their economic condition, changes in their contact with the community members and changes in their status. From our study it is found that women cannot go freely outside the home after becoming widows, because community looks at them suspiciously, but the case may differ from widow to widow. The young widows do not participate actively in auspicious occasions like marriage and birth ceremonies. They will watch the ceremonies. But as time passes they start participating in their family.

In the present study an analysis of the widows' participation in society has been undertaken. A widow's social participation implies her life outside the home. It includes her relations with her personal friends, neighbours in addition to her family members and husband's.

The problems of integration of widows in Veerashaiva community in the context of changing social order was discussed. Inspite of all the legal freedom guaranteed in the constitution and by the law, the position of women even after 45 years of independence has not changed much. Women are constantly being victimised and exploited by society. They are the victims of double exploitation by virtue of their being single.

Dual role of both men and women and in the process face a lot of problems. Even though Raja Ram Mohan Roy struggled for the abolition of child marriage, the stress and strain of widows are continuing. Due to many changes in economic order and joint family the problems of widows of any community will be same at least for the first ten years. The problems that the widows face are economic, social, health and emotional. They are interrelated and the degree of their seriousness varies with the widow's age, economic condition, family structure, religious norms etc. As the integration of widows in the context of changing order is concerned, this study found that, the attitudes of society towards them are liberalising, through modernization, urbanization, industrialization, employment and educational opportunities have brought changes in their life. The Veerashaiva widows are little bit free in decision making, meeting the relatives and friends, deciding the education of their children, moving out of the houses as compared to the widows of other communities.

Another important observation is that a review of social legislation pertaining to widows' rights and responsibilities, and examining the level of awareness of women of the legal rights which have been made available for them and especially for widows is attempted. It has been assumed that there is a positive relationship between the level of education and that of awareness of legal rights. Legal rights, like inheritance, (property rights) law pertaining to providing job of their husband to them, law pertaining to death registration, share given in father's property, awareness regarding widow remarriage act of 1856, law pertaining to widow pension are in vogue since independence and have been discussed. But these rights seem to have made little impact and yet to permeate the Hyderabad Karnataka region as the bulk of the respondents appear to, be absolutely ignorant of their legal rights. It is also attempted to examine widow's opinions and suggestions towards, providing educational facilities, rehabilitation of widows, provision for widow remarriage, removal of restrictions on widows, providing employment opportunities for widows. The analysis of the data revealed that widows favour all provisions. Favourable attitude has been found more among educated widows rather than among tradition-minded widows. The important findings of the study are as follows:

1. The findings pertaining to the demographic characteristics of the Veerashaiva widows of Gulbarga indicate that the highest (27.2%) percentage of widows belong to the age group of 51-60 years and the lowest numbers of (0.8%) widows belong to the age group of 10-20 years.
2. The findings pertaining to the subcaste of widows indicate that the highest percentage (36.0%) of widows come from Diksha Sub-caste while the

lowest(0.4%) percentage from Kudavakkligas and Hugars. This is an account of the highest percentage of Diksha Veerashaivas constituting the total population of the community.

3. With regard to the age of the respondents at the time of marriage, the study reveals that nearly 75% of the respondents age at the time of marriage was below 15 years. On the other hand most of the respondents' husbands married below 25 years.
4. With regard to the widows who started working after widowhood due to sheer economic necessity it is found that a little over half of them (46.4%) started working. It is significant to note that a greater number of widows whose husband's were only the earning members of the family started working. A very less number (4%) of widows engaged in their husbands' job itself. A majority of widows are helped by their parents/friends in getting the employment.
5. With regard to the type of family in which widows are staying indicates that majority of (63.8%) them are staying in joint families. While 37.2% are living in nuclear families.
6. As high as 62% of the widows have stated that they are living with their children.
7. The Study also reveals that a majority of the widows (99.6%) did not favour the idea of remarriage. Only one (0.4%) widow showed her favourable attitude towards remarriage.
8. With regard to the widows and their relation with husbands, the findings suggest that, majority of (68.8%) widows maintained good relations and only 4% of widows have bad relations.
9. As far as the integration of widows within the family is concerned about 58 percent of widows are well integrated because they do not feel insecure after the death of their husbands.

10. With regard to the widows and their in-laws' relations, the study reveals that, majority of the (89.6%) widows have undergone the stiffness of their in-laws which disfacilitated for their better integration.
11. As regards the resuming of normal work by widows within the family, the findings reveal that the highest percentage of (44.8%) widows resumed their normal work within 3 months as a result of the advice of elder members of the family, friends, neighbours and children.
12. Family is regarded as a better tool for integration of widows. Like in-laws' family, the parental family also plays an important role in the process of integration. The study reveals that most of the widows received sympathetic treatment from their parents.
13. As regards the roles played by widows in the family, the study shows that almost all widows were playing dual roles in the family as a part of integration.
14. As regards the integration of widows within the neighbourhood, the findings show that a considerable number of widows maintained earlier relations with them, and the social emotional support from them helped for their integration
15. With regard to the educational level of the deceased husbands, the findings reveal that a majority of deceased husbands(25.2%) were educated upto primary level. In support of this it may be stated that majority (23.2%) percent of the husbands were agriculturists. And 46 percent husbands' income was medium (Rs. 10,001-30,000)
16. With regard to the economic participation and integration of widows, the findings suggest that widows belonging to different age groups, young

and middle widows have faced more economic problems for integration than the aged widows. About 69.6% widows were getting financial support from their family members. This seeking of financial support shows that the death of the husband leads to a financial problem because he is the major earner of the family.

17. The Study pertaining to the share given in father's property reveals that very less number of widows(12%) got share in their natal family. While 66.8% widows got share in their marital property as a part of economic support to them. Majority of widows (72.4%) were receiving economic support from their children, and social support from parents, service support from neighbours, and about 32% of widows were getting various kinds of financial support from the Government. In support to this, about 78 percent widows' family expenditure was cut down drastically.

18. With regard to the religious participation and integration of widows, the findings indicate that, Veerashaivas do not distinguish between man and woman in religious matters, they regard woman as having equal religious status. They do not put restrictions on the performance of religious rituals even after their widowhood. A significant majority of (94%) of them started performing as much rituals as performed before their widowhood. Over 82.4 percent performed prayers daily as a part of religious activity. About 81.2 percent widows faced a problem of religious participation for first 3 years. It is also noticed that, comparing to their earlier life a significant number of (39.2%) them started visiting to temples on festival days instead of visiting once in a week. And nearly half of (52%) them started attending the religious discourses after widowhood as a part of religious integration.

19. With regard to social participation and integration of widows the findings indicate that majority of widows were meeting their friends, relatives once a month. But on the other hand 73.2% widows were not going out more frequently even when their husbands were alive.
20. An analysis of the attending the social functions by widows, a significant majority of (68.8%) them started attending the social functions after 2 years.
21. With regard to the problems faced by widows, the findings indicate that a significant majority of the widows (87.2%) were facing a problem of lack of companionship. Nearly half of them are facing the financial problems.
22. With regard to the awareness of respondents regarding the inheritance of property, the findings reveal that majority (88.4%) of the widows are aware of the legislation pertaining to property inheritance.
23. An analysis of the awareness of share given in father's property, the study reveals that nearly half of (58%) them are aware of the Share given in fathers property. Nearly 45.6 percent widows are also aware of Widow Remarriage Act of 1856. While more than half (54.4%) of them are ignorant about the law. A significant majority of (88.8%) them are aware of the assistance given by the Government as widow pension. Nearly half of them (56.8%) are unaware of the law pertaining to the death registration. As regards awareness of respondents of legal rights education plays an important role in keeping pensions abreast with the developments and those who are more educated will be more aware and conscious of their rights and duties. With regard to the opinions and suggestions towards providing educational facilities for widows, provision for widow remarriage removal or restrictions put forth on widows, providing

employment opportunities for widows, the findings reveal that irrespective of their status they are unanimous on the point of providing education to women, about 54.8 percent widows suggested provision for widow remarriage, a significant majority of (90%) them suggested for removal of restrictions put forth on widows, suggestion of widows for providing employment opportunity seems to be genuine and worth taking note of. The Government should come forward to create opportunities for them to earn their daily bread.

6.1 Recommendations and Resolutions for Better Integration of Widows

- A thorough inquiry should be instituted by both the central and the state Governments into the poor state of affairs prevailing in the widows living in different parts of the country, especially at Hyderabad Karnataka Region which is very backward in Karnataka.
- There should be reservation of jobs for widows in Government services, with relaxation of age.
- Vocational training facilities for developing and improving skills be created along with job opportunities for widows.
- The efforts should be made to create awareness among widows about their rights.
- Inheritance of property rights to the deceased husband's property should be given to the widow.
- Reservation of flats in the housing scheme for widows and allotment on priority basis.
- A widow should have a right of residence in her parents-in-laws' home.
- As in Government service, a man's job should be given either to his widow or children in the private sector too.

- Young, illiterate and poor widows should be given opportunities by voluntary organisation and Government to improve their education and professional competence to enable them to take remunerative work.
- Information regarding the different welfare schemes existing in different parts of the country should be made known to people through the mass media time.
- Community-based agencies should start "the widow to widow programme", i.e., a group of widows should reach out to recently widowed women and offer support in helping them to adjust to their new life.
- Government and policy makers should come forward to show the misuse and irregularities which aggravate the lot of widows.
- Efforts should be made to remove the malpractices which accompany the payment of pension or other benefits to the widows. The Karnataka Government has started the practice of paying pension of Rs. 50.00 per month to an illiterate widow. But the middlemen can cheat and engage in misappropriation depriving the widow in the process. Such frauds should be removed and an improved procedure should be devised to see that the widow gets the pension without fail and without any loss in the process.

6.2 Areas of Future Research

- Various kinds of problems faced by different categories of widows like working, non-working, educated and uneducated, rich, poor and middle class should be studied in detail, which might help in formulating our welfare scheme network specially in rural areas.

- Similar studies in different communities may be conducted to make generalization about the impact of widowhood on the individual and society, which may perhaps help in redesigning our welfare' programmes.
- Indepth studies should be conducted covering not only widows but also widows. so as to know clearly their feelings about widowhood and the problems faced by them.
- Variations in widowhood from nation to nation, from state to state and between country and city should be studied in order to understand the future trend of widowhood in this country.
- A case study of students who have suffered the loss of a parent some years ago should be conducted to know how their life has been affected by this loss.

Appendix

Trends of Widowhood in India

The data presented in the table given below depicts the prevalence of widowhood in India and karnataka from 1951 to 1981.

Table A.l: Prevalence of Widowhood in India and Karnataka

Years	*India*		*Karnataka*	
	Males	*Females*	*Males*	*Females*
1951	5.00	12.80	4.31	15.36
1961	3.69	10.82	3.16	12.36
1971	4.14	12.67	2.27	10.35
1981	2.43	08.06	1.82	9.59

Source: Census of India, 1951, 1961, 1971 & 1981.

In India from 1951 to 1961 the percentage of widowhood remains more or less stable around 12 percent. However, in 1981 this figure has come down by four points. On the other hand there is a steady decline in the ere is a steady decline in the percentage of widowhood which was 5 percent in 1951 1951 and has come down to 2.4 percent in 1981. In karnataka also the percentage of widowhood of widowhood was 15.4 percent in 1951 has come down to 9.6 percent in 1981, while the percentage of widowhood in 1951 was 4.3 has down to 1.8 percent in 1981.

The prevalence of widowhood is determined by the decline in mortality, sex differentials in mortality in adult and old ages and the incidence of marriage of widowed persons.

Widows have been outnumbering widowers as can be seen in Table 2 because females live longer than males. Also men usually marry women quite younger in age and lesser widows remarry, the sexes differential immortality in late adulthood and old age are universally favourable to women. These factors cause increase in the incidence of widowhood.

Table A.2: Age and Sex Specific Prevalence of Widowhood in India 1961, 1971 and 1981

Age group	*Prevalence of Widowhood*					
	Male			*Female*		
	1961	*1971*	*1981*	*1961*	*1971*	*1981*
10-14	0.07	0.04	0.02	0.13	0.05	0.03
15-19	0.29	0.02	0.09	0.52	0.34	0.21
20-24	0.90	0.58	0.38	1.29	0.88	0.69
25-29	1.67	1.25	0.78	2.89	1.94	1.50
32-34	2.61	1.25	0.78	2.89	1.94	1.50
35-39	3.67	2.66	1.94	11.14	7.04	5.42
42-44	5.98	4.43	3.31	20.66	14.38	10.86
45-49	8.24	5.90	4.46	28.84	20.66	15.96
50-54	12.37	9.64	7.34	45.47	36.60	29.71
55-59	15.53	12.07	8.97	50.24	41.22	31.79
60-64	21.83	17.15	14.11	69.62	62.41	56.05
65-69	25.87	20.41	17.84	71.84	64.59	58.55
70 +	36.10	30.45	27.04	84.38	80.36	77.55
Age not stated	2.92	-	1.53	5.64	-	5.58

Source: *(1)* Social and cultural tables, 1961 Census of India. *(2)* Country monograph series -10; Population of India (UN) *(3)* Family welfare year book, 1982-83.

Table A.3: Age Specific Death Rates by Sex in India 1970 and 1980

Age group	*Specific Death Rates*			
	Male		*Female*	
	1970	*1980*	*1970*	*1980*
0-4	51.7	40.1	55.1	43.5
5-9	4.6	3.3	5.0	4.0
10-14	2.0	1.7	2.4	1.7
15-19	2.5	2.0	3.7	2.9
20-24	2.9	2.3	4.6	3.8
25-29	3.3	2.2	4.9	4.0
30-34	4.0	8.4	5.2	3.6
35-39	4.7	4.7	5.7	4.6
40-44	8.0	7.2	5.9	5.5
45-49	11.0	9.6	8.0	7.3
50-54	17.9	14.6	12.9	10.4
55-59	25.5	21.5	16.5	16.7
60-64	42.7	35.0	31.4	27.3
70 +	117.1	98.5	104.0	85.3
All ages	15.8	12.4	15.6	12.4

Source: SRS Bulletin.

There has been a steady decline in the levels of mortality in all the age groups for both the sexes, as could be seen in Table A.3. The female death rates are not only lesser than that of males from early adulthood onwards but also steadily widens in margin between the sexes as age progress.

Table A.4: Percentage of Widowed and Widowered by Rural/Urban Status for India at 1961, 1971 and 1981

Widowed/Widowered	*1961*	*1971*	*1981*
Widowed			
1. Total	10.82	8.86	8.06
2. Rural	11.01	9.03	8.23
3. Urban	9.90	8.15	7.46
Widowered			
1. Total	3.69	2.94	2.43
2. Rural	3.90	3.19	2.71
3. Urban	2.76	1.97	1.56 1

Source: Census of India 1961, part-II - *(i)*, social and cultural Tables, census of India 1971, series 1 India, part II-C *(ii)*, social and cultural tables, reports and Tables based on 5 percent sample data, series 1, India part II- special census of India, 1981.

It is noticed from the Table A. 4 that as compared to the widowered the percentage of widowed is high both in rural and urban India.

Table A.5: Pattern of Widowhood by Religion in India, 1981

Age group	*Hindus*		*Muslims*		*Christians*		*Sikhs*		*Buddhists*	
	A	*B*	*A*	*B*	*A*	*B*	*A*	*B*	*A*	*B*
10-14	0.87	0.04	0.45	0.12	2.25	0.03	2.54	0.07	3.41	0.15
15-19	1.31	0.43	2.02	1.13	2.51	0.41	0.57	0.13	3.07	1.17
20-24	1.66	1.31	2.46	2.47	2.00	1.39	0.59	0.71	3.25	2.59
25-29	2.42	2.09	2.86	2.78	2.59	2.42	0.84	1.16	3.28	2.62
30-34	4.04	3.02	4.34	3.49	4.28	3.24	1.75	2.13	4.74	3.07
35-39	6.27	4.45	6.30	4.59	6.48	4.67	3.03	3.04	8.73	4.42
40-44	11.79	7.13	12.80	7.29	12.41	6.63	5.34	4.76	12.10	6.67
45-49	16.81	9.18	17.36	8.60	15.84	8.92	7.77	6.43	20.18	9.74
50 +	49.36	72.34	48.92	69.55	44.37	72.79	31.50	81.57	51.20	69.57
All	15.73	100.0	15.02	100.0	16.52	100.0	10.61	100.0	17.49	100.0

Mean age at widowhood:

35.08*, 22998343 34.29*, 2767996 34.43*, 631645 33.89*, 329211 32.67*, 217716

(84.49) (10.17) (2.32) (1.21) (0.80)

Source: Census of India, 1981. Series-1. India, part-II-special, Report and tables based on 5 percent sample data.

4*' refers to mean age of widowhood.

Figures in the brackets refers to the percentages of total widows.

Table A.5 depicts the pattern of widowhood by religion in India. They were 84.49 percentage among Hindus and 10.17 among Muslims. They were 2.32 and 2.19, among Sikhs they were 1.21 and 1.78 percent and among Buddhists the percentages were 0.80 and 0.71 percent. It is observed

Table A.6: Percentage of Widows and Ever Married Women by Age and Educational Level 1981 India

Age group	*Illiterate*		*Literate*							
			Below middle		*Above middle*		*Below graduate*		*Graduate & above*	
	A	*B*	*A*	*B*	*A*	*B*	*A*	*B*	*A*	*B*
10-14	0.91	0.09	0.78	0.10	0.82	0.10	0.59	0.01	0.00	0.00
15-19	1.52	0.64	1.27	1.18	0.73	1.51	0.58	1.03	0.31	0.09
20-24	1.94	1.33	1.77	3.39	1.05	5.15	0.72	5.45	0.31	2.67
25-29	2.67	1.83	2.58	4.60	1.83	7.99	1.12	8.76	0.49	7.50
30-34	4.29	2.71	4.02	5.39	3.05	8.40	2.04	10.34	1.42	14.10
35-39	6.55	3.98	5.86	6.88	4.33	8.39	3.15	9.94	2.20	11.72
40-44	12.30	6.72	9.75	8.16	7.78	9.57	6.31	11.93	4.58	14.08
45-49	17.17	8.19	15.29	10.68	12.38	11.22	10.17	12.05	7.60	12.51
50 & above	49.93	74.51	41.06	59.62	33.16	47.67	27.10	40.49	20.75	37.34
All ages	17.73	100.00	9.75	100.00	5.06	100.00	3.34	100.00	2.17	100.00

Mean age at widowhood:
37.74*, 24498993 34.60*, 214316 35.29*, 352693 36.19*, 192511 37.36*, 32565
(90.00) (7.88)(1.30) (0.70) (0.12)
Source: As mentioned in Table A.5
'*' refers to mean age at widowhood
Figures in the brackets refers to the percentage of total widows.

that among all the religions Sikhs had minimum proportion of widows and Buddhists had maximum proportion of widows. It is also noticed that the differences in the proportion widows by age were negligible among all the religions except Sikhs.

It is noticed in Table A.6 that 24.5 million, i.e., 90 percent of total widows were reported to be illiterates, whereas the corresponding number among ever-married was 79. The percentage of widows among literate is 7.88. 1.30 percent were educated upto middle level. 0.70 were educated upto matriculation and 0.12 were graduate and above.

Table A.7: Mean Age at Widowhood of those Getting Widowed by Age, 45 India and Karnataka, 1901-11 to 1971-81

Decades	*India*	*Karnataka*
1901-1911	31.2	29.5
1911-1921	29.8	25.5
1921-1931	34.1	33.0
1931-1941	28.8	32.2
1941-1951	32.2	33.1
1951-1961	34.0	36.5
1961-1971	35.1	34.7
1971-1981	36.2	35.9

Source: Agarwala S.N., India's population problem, Tata McGraw-Hill publication, 1977, Delhi.

Figure upto 1951 include divorced, and refer to old Mysore.

Source: Data upto 1951 census of India 1951 Mysore Vol. 14, 1954, Bangalore. 1961 census of India, 1961, Mysore Vol. 11, part-II C(l), Social and Cultural Tables, 1966, Delhi. 1971 census of India, 1971, Series 14, part-II C(2), Social and Cultural Tables, 1981, Delhi. 1981 census of India, 1981, series 9, Karnataka part-II, Special report and tables based on 5 percent sample data, 1984, Delhi.

It is observed from the Table A.7 that the mean age at widowhood is varying from 1901 to 1941, whereas, since 1951 the number is increasing in India. While in

Karnataka the mean age at widowhood is varying from 1901 to 1981. In Karnataka the high proportion of mean age at widowhood is found in the decade 1951-1961.

Table A.8: Percentage of Widowed Females for India and Karnataka in 1961, 1971 and 1981

Place	*Percentage of Widowed Females*		
	1961	*1971*	*1981*
India	10.82	8.86	8.06
Karnataka	12.36	10.35	9.59

Source: Census of India 1961, part-II C(l), Social and cultural tables, census of India, 1971, series-I. India: part-II C(2), Social and cultural tables, reports and tables based on 5 percent sample data, series-I, India, part-II special census of India, 1981.

It is noticed in Table A.8 that, the percentage of widowed females in India is with decreasing trend from 1961 to 1981. The same situation is observed in K Karnataka in the same period. The percentage of widowed females is declined from 10 percent to 8 percent in India. While, during the same period it is declined from 12 percent to 9 percent in Karnataka.

Table A.9: Percentage of widowed females by residential status for India and Karnataka in 1961, 1971 and 1981

	Percentage of widowed females					
	Rural			*Urban*		
Place	*1961*	*1971*	*1981*	*1961*	*1971*	*1981*
India	11.01	9.03	8.23	9.19	8.15	7.46
Karnataka	12.81	10.77	9.95	10.77	9.00	8.67

Source: Census of India 1961, part-II C(l), Social and cultural tables, census of India, 1971, series-I. India: part-II C(2), Social and cultural tables, reports and tables based on 5 percent sample data, series-I, India, part-II special census of India, 1981.

As far the percentage of widowed females by residential status in India and Karnataka is concerned, Table A.9 shows that both in rural and urban areas the percentage is declined from 1961 to 1981. In India during 1961 and 1981 the prevalence of widowhood among females declined from 11 percent to 8 percent in rural area and 9 percent to 7 percent in urban area. While during the same period the prevalence of widowed females in Karnataka declined ,from 12 percent to 9 percent in rural area and 10 percent to 8 percent in urban area.

Bibliography

Abrahams, Ruby. 1972: Mutual Help for the widowed, *Social Work,* Vol. 17, No. 5, pp. 54-61.

Abraham, M. Francis. 1988: *Modern Sociological Theory, An Introduction,* Bombay, Oxford University Press.

Abbott, J.E. 1930: *My Story: The Autobiography of a Hindu Widow,* London, GP Putnam's Sons.

Agarwala, S.N. 1967: Age of Widowhood and Length of fertile union of India (*Demographia,* Vol. 10, No. 2)

Agarwala, S.N. 1965: Age of widowhood in India, Delhi (Mimeographed) Institute of Economic Growth.

Agarwala, S.N. 1962: Widow remarages in India, *Medical Digest,* Vol. 30, No. 10, pp. 548-557.

Agarwala, S.N. 1968: Widowhood Age and Length of Fertile Union. Budapest world views of population problems, Hungarian Academy of Sciences.

Agarwala, S.N. 1967: Widow Remarriages in some Rural Areas of Northern India. *Demography* Vol. 4, No. 1, pp. 126-134.

Ajit Kumar Ray, 1985: *Widows are not for Burning,* New Delhi, ABC Publishing House.

Agarwal, A.G. (Ed) 1978: *Poverty, Deprivation and Intelligence,* New Delhi, Criterion Publication.

Albert Caevan, J. Henry Korson. Sep. 1972: The Widowed who live Alone; An Examination of Social and Demographic factors. *Social Forces,* Vol. 51, No. 1.

Allen, R.E. (Ed.) 1984: *The Oxford Dictionary of Current English,* Delhi, Oxford University Press.

Ali Khan Mumtaz, Noor Aysha, 1982: *Status of Rural Women in India,* New Delhi, Uppal Publishing house.

Allen, Michael and Mukherjee, S.N. (Ed.) 1982: *Women in India and Nepal,* Canberra, ANU Publications.

(Mrs.) Almelkar, P. 1987 (Mar): Widowhood Community Attitud es and perception. Dharwad, Janata Shikshana Samiti, National Seminor on Widowhood in India

Altekar, A.S. 1956: *The Postion of Women in Hindu Civilization,* Banaras, Motilal Banarsidas.

Anderson, Trudy B. 1984: Widowhood as a Life Transition—Its Impact on Kinship Ties. *Journal of Marriage and the Family,* No. 1, pp. 105 -114.

Annual Meeting Scientific Proceedings. 1967: Bereavement, *British Medical Journal,* Vol. 3, No. 1, pp. 232-233.

Ammal Subbalakshmi, R.S. 1970 (June): A saviour of widows, *Social Welfare,* Vol. XVII; No. 3.

Aradhya, B.M.M. 1987 (Dec.): What it means to be a widow, *Social Welfare,* Vol. XXXIV; No. 9., pp. 2-3.

Arens, D.A. 1982-83: Widowhood and Well-being: An Examination of Sex differences within a Causal Model. *International Journal of Aging and Human Development,* Vol. 15, No. 1.

Arling, G. 1976: The elderly widow and her family, Neighbours and friends, *Journal of Marriage and Family,* Vol. 38 (Aug.).

Apte, Usha M. 1978: *The Sacrament of Marriage in Hindu Society from Vedic period to Dharmasastras*, Delhi, Aajanta.

Athavale, Parvati, 1930: *My Story—The Autography of Hindu*

Widow, New York, G.P. Putnam.

Baidyanath Sarswati 1983 (June): The Kashivasi widows, *Man in India,* Vol. 65, No. 2, pp. 107-120.

Bajpai, S.R. (Dr.) 1972: *Methods of Social Survey and Research,* Kanpur, Kitab Ghar, Fifth Edn.

Balsubramanyam, V. 1970: A Saviour of Widows—A Profile on R.S. Subbalakshmi Ammal. *Social Welfare,* Vol. XVII. No. 3, pp. 27.

Balasubramanian, C. 1976: *The Status of Women in Tamil Nadu during the Sangam Age,* Madras University of Madras Press.

Banerjee, Gooroodas. 1984: *Hindu Law of Marriage and Stridhana,* Delhi, Mittal Publications.

Bankoff, B.A. 1983: Social support and adaptation to widowhood. *Journal of Marriage and the Family,* Vol. 45. (4th Nov) pp. 827-839.

Baron, Omar and Rolf, Ehrenfels. 1947: *Mother Right in India,* Hyderabad, Oxford University Press.

Batra, Sushma, 1981: *Social Integration of the Blind (A Study in Delhi)* New Delhi, Concept Publishing Company.

Barse, Sheela, 1980 (Sept., 14): I shall pretend that I am not (*Illustrated Weekly of India*) Vol. 101, No. 37.

Benson, Leonard 1971: *The Family Bond—Marriage, Love and Sex in America,* New-York, Random House Inc.

Bernard, Farber (Ed) 1966: *Kinship and Family Organisation,* New-York, John Wiley and sons. Inc.

Berardo, F.M. 1967: Social adaptation to widowhood among rural-ruban aged population. *Washington Agricultural Experiment Station Bulletin* 687(Dec)

Berardo, Felix M. 1968: Widowhood Status in the United States perspective on a Neglected Aspect of the Family Life Cycle, *The Family Coordinator,* Vol 17 (July) No. 3, pp. 191-203.

Berardo, Felix M. 1970: Survivorship and Social Isolation: The case of the Aged widower, *The Family Coordinator.* Vol. 19, No. 1, pp. 11-25.

Bhate, G.C. 1907: *Permitting Widow-marriages*, Poona, Widow Marriage Association.

Bhagat, Rekha & P.N. Mathur 1989: *Mass Media and Farm Women*, New Delhi, Intellectual Publishing House.

Bhat, M. and R. Kanbargi, 1984 (Mar.): Estimating the incidence of Widow and Widow Re-marriage in India from Census Data, *Population Studies*.

Bharat, Shalini 1986: Single Parent Family in India: Issues and Implications, *The Indian Journal of Social Work*, Vol. XLVII, No. 1, pp. 55-65.

Bidarakoppa, G.S. 1971: Position and Problem of Hindu Widows, *Journal of the Karanataka University Social Sciences*, Vol. 7, pp. 76-82.

Bhim Raja. 1969: *Marriage and Hindu Widows*, (2ndEdn) Bombay, Indu Prakash Press.

Bhuler, G. (Trans) 1886: *Laws of Manu*, Delhi, Motilal Banarasidas.

Billington, Marry Frances 1973: *Woman in India: A Study of Medieval*, New Delhi, Amarko Book Agency.

Bhusan, Jamila Brij 1973: *War Widows Weekly Round Table*. July 1, pp. 26-30.

Bose, A.B. and Sen, M.L.A. 1966: Some Characterstics of the Widows in Rural Societies, *Man in India*, Vol. 46, No. 3, pp. 223-32.

Bock, Wilbur E., Irving L. Webber. (Feb. 1972): Suicide Among the Elderly: Isolating widowhood and Mitigation Alternatives, *Journal of Marriage and Family*, Vol. 34, No. 1.

Bottomore, T.B. 1979: *Sociology as Social Criticism*, New-Delhi. S.Chand and Company Ltd.

O'Brayant, Shirley L. 1988: Sibling Support and Older Widow's Well-being, *Journal of Marriage and the Family*, Vol. 50, No. 1, pp. 164-184.

Burbaker, T.H. 1985: *Later Life Families*, London, Sage Publications.

Burgess, Ernest W. and Locke, Hurvey J. 1945: *The Family from Institution to Companionship,* New York, American Book Co.

Caplan, Patricia, 1985: *Class and Gender in India: Women and their Organisations in a South Indian City,* London and New York, Tavistock Publications.

Caton, A.R. (Ed) 1930: *The Key Progress: A Survey of the Status and Condition of Woman in India,* London. Oxford University Press.

Chakraborthy, D.C. 1988: Changing customs of women in a near extinct race, in Bhowmick ed., *Development of Women and Children* Inter India Publications.

Chakravarty, A. 1975: Hindu widowhood, *Hinduism: Journal of the Bharat Sevashram Sangh,* Vol. 68, pp. 12-13.

Chamke, B.N. 1985: *The Heart of Virashaivism, Barsi Dist. Solapur,* Smt. S.B. Chamke, 1552/9 Agalgaon Road.

Chandrnshekhar Shivacharya (Dr) 1985: *Veerashaiva Asthtavarana—Vidnyana,* Guledgudd, (Karanataka) Amareshwarmath.

Chattopadhayay, Kamaladevi, 1983: *Indian Women's Battle for Freedom*. New Delhi, Abhinav Publications.

Chattopadhay, Aparna, 1975: Positions of widows in early medieval Inaia in the light of the Kathasarit Sagara, *Journal of Oriental Institute,* Vol. 24, No. 3-4, pp. 393-402.

Chekki, Danesh (Mar. 1991): The Status and Roles of Veerashaiva Women in Contemporary Society. Bangalore-Basava Samiti, Basava Bhavan. Sree Basaveshwara Road, Sree Basaveshwara Circle.

Chevan, Albert & J. Henry Korson, 1975 (Aug.): Living Arrangements of widows in the United States and Israel 1960 and 1961, *Demography,* Vol. 12, No. 3.

Chevan, Albert and Korson J. Henry 1972: The Widowed who Live Alone: An Examination of Social and Demographic Factors, *Social Forces,* Vol. 51, No. 1. pp. 45-53.

Chhabra, Rami 1975: Tragedy of the traditional Indian Widow, *Indian Express*, 11, pp. 1-2.

Cooperman, Irene G. Second Careers 1971: War Wives and Widows, *The vocational Guidance Quarterly*, Vol. 20, pp. 103-11.

Coser, A. Lewis 1971: *Master of Sociological Thought*, London: Harcourt Brace Iovanovich Publishers.

Cosneck, Bernard J. 1970: Family patterns of Older Widowed Jewish People, *The Family Coordinator*, Vol. 19, No. 2, pp. 365-373.

Crabtree, J.L. Displced homemaker 1980: Middle aged alone and broke, *Aging*, Nos. 303-304, pp. 17-20.

Cutlet, J.A. 1963: Integration a Social and Political Problem, *Cultural Form*.

Datta, V.N. 1988: *Sati Widow Burning in India*, New Delhi, Manohar Publications.

Dandavate, Premila; Ranjana Kumari and Verghese, Jamila 1989: *Widows Abandoned and Destitute Women in India*, New Delhi, Radiant Publishers.

Datta, N.K. 1938: Widow in ancient India, *Indian Historical Quarterly*, Vol. 14, No. 4.

Datta, Jatindra Mohan: Is Enforced Widowhood the only cause of the slower growth of the Bangalore Hindus.

Desai, A.R. 1967 (Mar): National Integration and Religion; *Sociological Bulletin*.

Desai, Murli 1987: Widow with main earning responsibility and care of their children, Dharwad, Janata Shikshana Samiti, National Seminor on Widowhood in India.

Dornne, Jacobson and Susons and Wadley 1986: *Women in India—Two Perspectives*, Delhi, Manohar Publications.

D'Souza Alfred. (Ed) 1980: *Women in Contemporary India and South Asia*, (2nd Edn) New Delhi, Manohar Publications.

Dubey, Bhagwant Rao, 1965 (Mar.): Widow Remarriage in Madhya Pradesh, *Man in India*, Vol. 45.

Duberman, Lucile 1977: *Marriage and other Alternatives* (2nd Edn.) New York, Praeger Publishers.

Dubios, Abbe D.V. 1906: *Hindu Manners, Customs and Ceremonies* (3rd Edn) Trans. by Henry K. Beauchamp. London, Oxford University Press.

Dulude, Louise 1978: Women and Aging—A report on the best of our lives. Ottawa, Advisory Council on the Status of Women.

Dutt, Ruby 1965: The Property Rights of Women in the Sutra Period, *The Modern Review,* Vol. CXVIII, No. 3, pp. 239-246.

Editor 1936: Mysore Widow Marriage Bill, *The Indian Social Reform,* June 20, p. 353.

Editor 1983: Legislation on Woman, *Social Welfare,* Vol. XXIX, No. 11-12, pp. 20.

Eliot, Thomas D. 1930: The Adjustive Behaviour of Bereved Families: A New Field For Research, *Social Forces,* Vol. 8, No. 4, pp. 543-549.

Eliot, Thomas D. 1932-33: A Step toward. The Social Psychology of Berravement, *Journal of Abnormal and Social Psychology,* Vol. 27, No. 3, pp. 380-390.

Eliot, Thomas D. 1943: ... of the Shadow of Death, *Annals of the American Academy of Political and Social Sciences,* Vol. 229, No. 1, pp. 94-95.

Eshleman J. Ross 1974: *The Family—An Introduction* (2nd Edn), Boston, Allyn and Bacon Inc.

Essex, Marilyn J. and Nam Sunghee 1987: Marital Status and Loneliness Among Older Women: The Differential Importance of Close Family and Friends, *Journal of Marriage and the Family,* Vol. 49, No. 1, pp. 93-106.

Felton, Monica 1966: *A Child Widow's Story,* London, Victor Gallancz.

Fritz, Mary 1929: A Study of Widowhood, *Sociology and Social Research,* Vol. XIV, No. 1, pp. 553-561.

Fuller, Marcus B. (Mrs) 1984: *The Wrong of Inaian Womenhood,* New Delhi, Inter-India Publications.

Gandhi, M.K. 1964: *The Role of Women,* Bombay, Bharatiya Vidya Bahavan.

George, M. Beal, Ronald C. Powers E. Walter Coward Jr. 1971: *Sociological perspectives of Domestic Development*, Ames, Iowa, The Iowa State University Press.

Gerald, L.R. 1977: *Marriage in Changing World*, New York, John Wiley and Sons Co.

Gerald, L.R. 1979: *The Family in Social Context*, New York, Oxford University Press.

Ghosh, Jogesh Chandra 1982: *Hindu Woman of India*, Delhi, Bimala Publishing House.

Ghureye, G.S. 1969: *Caste and Race in India*, Bombay, Popular Prakashan.

Ghureye, G.S. 1936: Marriage and Widowhood in India: A study of a middle class sample of 3400 marriages, *Marriage Hygiene*, Vol. 2, No. 3, pp. 258-270.

Girija Khanna (Dr.) Mariamma A. 1978: *Indian Women Today*, New Delhi, Vikas Publishing House Pvt. Ltd.

Gold Thorpe, John H.: Social inequality and Social Integration, in Dorothy Wedderburn (Edn.) *Poverty Inequality and Class Structure in Modern Britain*.

Giddens, Anthony and Jonathan H. Turner 1987: *Social Theory Today*, Polity Press.

Gill, Kulwant (Dr.): *Hindu Women's Right to Poverty in India*, New Delhi, Deep & Deep Publications.

Gordon, Michael, Whelan Brendan, Vaughan Richard 1981: Old age and loss of Household Headship: A National Irish Study, *Journal or Marriage and Family*, Vol. 43.

Ghosh, S.K.: *Indian Women Through the Ages*, New Delhi, Ashish Publishing House.

Gore, M.S. 1968: *Urbanization and Family Change*, Bombay, Popular Prakashan.

Guha, Amalendu 1979: Great nationalism, little Nationalism and problem of Integration A tentative view, *Economic and Political Weekly*, Vol. 14, No. 7&8.

Gulati, Saroj: *Women and Society Northern India in 11th and 12th Centuries*, Delhi, Chanakya Publications.

Harichandran, C. (Dr.) (1985, Jun. 1-15): Socio-Economic

Conditions of Widows A study, *Yojana*, Vol. 26, No. 10, pp. 11-12.

Hastings, James (Edn.) 1953: *Encyclopedia of Religion and Ethics*, New-York Pub. Edinburgh, T. and T. Clark, Vol. 8, No. 3.

Harvey, C.D. and Bennes, E.G. 1986: Correlates of Morale among candian Widowed Persons. Paper presented at the International Sociological Association, New Delhi.

Harvey, C.D. and H.M. Bahr 1974: Widowhood, Morale and Affiliation, *Journal of Marriage and the Family*, Vol. 36, 1st Feb.

Hate, Chandrakala A. 1984: *Hindu Women and Her Future*, Bombay, New Book Co Ltd.

Hill, K.: Estimating Adult Mortality levels from information on widowhood. *Population Studies*.

Hinch Cliffe D. 1973: Widows dower-debt in India, *Islam and Modern Age*, Vol. 4, No. 3.

Hopata, Lelena Z. 1990: Widowhood, Disorganization and Reorganization and life Grame Works. Jaipur: Arihant Publishers Book: *Violence Against Women*.

Hurber, Joan (Edn.) 1973: *Changing Women in a Changing Society*, Chicago, The University of Chicago Press.

Hyman, Herbert H. 1983: *Of Time and Widowhood—Nationwide Studies of Enduring Efforts*, Durham Duke Press.

Ihinger, Marilyn-Tallman and Kay Pasley: *Remarriage* (Gopal Book/Ws) Family studies Text series 7.

Ila Mukherje: *Social status of North Indian Women 1526-1707 AD*, Shivalal Agarwala and Company Educational Publishers.

Irving, M. Zetlin 1987: *Rethinking in Sociology*, Jaipur, Rawat Publications.

Ishwaran, K. 1983: *Religion and Society among the Lingayats of South India*, New-Delhi, Vikas Publishing House Pvt Ltd.

Jamila, Brij Bhushan 1973 (July): War Widows. *Weekly Round Table,* pp. 26-30.

Jangam, R.T. (Dr) 1985 (June & Sept): Basaveshwara and the status of women. Bangalore, Basavasamiti, *Basava Journal,* Vol. 9 & 10, No. 4 & 1.

Kalhan, Promilla 1978: Married in India, divorced abroad (*The Hindustan Times,* pp. 1.1)

Kamat, A.R. 1963: (The) Decline in death rate and the effect on the widowhood. (*Sociological Bulletin,* pp. 18-31).

Kamalani, Ratu 1978: Memories of widowhood. (*Eve's Weekly,* pp. 36-37).

Kanvi, C.S. (Ed.) 1977: *Women Her Problems and Her Achivements,* Dharwad, karanataka University Press.

Kapadia, K.M. 1958: *Marriage and Family in India,* (2nd Edn.) London, Oxford University Press.

Karve, Irawati 1953: *Kinship Organisation in India,* Bombay, Asia Publishing house.

Karve, Neera 1956: The lot of a widow, *Social Welfare,* Vol. 3, No. 4.

Katti, A.P and H.V. Nagesh 1984 (Jan): A Socio-Economic Study of Widows, *Journal of Economic Research,* Vol. 19, No. 7.

Katti, A.P and H.V. Nagesh: A Study of Widows, *Journal of Institute of Economic Research.*

Kaur, Indrajeet 1983: *Status of Hindu Women in India,* Allahabad, Chugh Publications.

Kelpharat, William M. 1981: *The Family, Society and Individuals* (5th Edn), Boston, Houghton Mifflin Co.

Kimball, Young 1952: *Personality and Problems of Adjustment* (2nd Edn). London, Routledge and Kegan Paul Ltd.

Kiran, Devendra 1985: *Status and Position of Women in India,* New Delhi, Vikas Publishing House Pvt Ltd.

Kitchlu, T.N. 1979: Profile of Widows in Delhi. (*Social Work,* Vol. 25, No. 10, pp. 23-35).

Kripalani, Rajika 1974 (July): Nobody Wants a widow. (*Radiance,* pp. 5)

Krishnakumari, N.S. 1987: *Status of Single Women in India,* New Delhi, Uppal Publishing House.

Kulshreshtah, Indra Noopur 1989: *Women's Studies in School Education: A New Perspective,* Sterling Publishers Private Ltd.

Kumar, Swamiji 1960: *Mirror of Virashivism,* Dharwar, Navakalyana Math Prakashan.

Lakshmi, C.S. 1984: *Women in Society—The Face Behind the Mask,* New Delhi, Vikas Publishing House.

Lakhanpal, C. 1935: The Hindu widow (In *Our Cause,* Ed. by Sk. K. Nehru. Allahabad, Kitabistan, pp. 268-86)

Landekar, Werner S. 1952: Types of integration and their Measurement. *American Journal of Sociology,* Vol. 56.

Landis, Judon T. and Londis Marg G. (Edn) 1953: *Readings in Marriage and the Family,* New York, Prentice Hall Inc.

Landis, Paul H. 1954: *Your Marriage and Family living* (2nd Edn) New York, McGraw Hill Book Co.

Landis, Paul H. 1954: *Making the Most of Marriage* (2nd Edn.) New York, Appleton Century Crofts Inc.

Leo, Stole 1956 (Dec): Social integration and Certain Corollarien. *American Sociological Review,* Vol. 21:6.

Lopata Helena Znaniecki 1981: Widowhood and Husband Sanctification, *Journal of Marriages and Family,* Vol. 43.

Lopata, Helena Znaniecki 1978 (May): Contributions of Extended Families to the suport Systems of Metropolitan Area Widows, Limitations of the Modified Kin Network, *Journal of Marriage and Family,* Vol. 40, No. 2.

Lopata, Helena Z. 1973: *Widowhood in a American City,* Cambridge, Schenkman Pbulishing Co.

Lopata, Helena Z. 1969: Loneliness: Forms and Components *Social Problems,* Vol. 17, No. 2, pp. 248-262.

Lopata, Helena Z. 1978: The Absence of Community Resources in suport Systems of Urban widows. *The Family Coordinator,* Vol. 27, No. 4, pp. 383-394.

Lopata, Helena Z. 1970: The Social Involvemen of Americal Widows. *American Behavioural Scientist,* Vol. 14, No. 1, pp. 41-57.

Lopamudra 1983 (Mar): *The Plight of Widows Social Welfare,* Central College Library, Bangalore.

Little, Kenneth 1973: *African Women in Towns: An aspect of African's Social Revolution London,* New York, Cambridge University Press, Cambridge.

Lukose, A. 1978: Facing Widowhood, *Eves Weekly.* (Aug 12-18) p. 35.

Madan, T.N. (Dr.) 1965: *Family and Kinship,* Bombay, Asia Publishing House.

Madhawadas, Rugunathdas 1890: *Story of a Widow Remarriage,* Bombay, S.K. Khambata & Co.

Malabari, Behramji M. 1887: *Infant Marriage and enforced Wdiowhood in India,* Bombay, Voice of India.

Mandelbaum, David G. 1984: *Society in India,* Bombay, Second Edn. Popular Prakashan.

Mankekar, Kamala 1987 (Dec): Murder in the name of Religion; *Social Welfare,* Vol. 34, No. 9.

Marris, Peter 1958: *Widows and Their Families,* London, Routledge and Kegan Paul Ltd.

Martindale, Don 1990: *The Nature and Types of Sociological Theory,* Jaipur, Rawat Publications.

Martinson, F. 1970: *Family in Society,* New York. Doddmead.

Mary, Corcoran 1979: The Economic Consequences of Martial Dissolution for women in the middle years. *Sex Roles,* Vol. 5, No. 3.

Mehta, Manubhai N. 1961: Widow Marriage and Hindu Society. *The Indian Social Reform,* Vol. XLVL. No. 49, p. 775.

Menon, Lakshmi N. 1973: Indian Women Since Independence, *Indian and Foreign Review,* Vol. 10, No. 2.

Merton, R.K. 1968: *Social Theory and Social Structure,* New Delhi, Amerind Publishing Co. Pvt. Ltd.

Malledevaru, H.P. (Dr.) 1973: *Essentials of Virasaivism,* Bombay, Bharatiya Vidya Bahavan.

Moghe, Dev Vrunda 1978 (Aug.): Widowhood today: A long way from the dark past. (*Eve's Weekly,* pp. 33-34).

Mehra, Rekha K. Saradamoni 1983: *Women and Rural Transformation,* New Delhi, Concept Publishing Company.

Mitter, Dwarka Nath 1984: *The Position of Women in Hindu Law,* Delhi, Inter-India Publications.

Mitchell, Duman G. 1968: Routledge and Paul K. (Edn) 1968: *A Dictionary of Sociology.* London.

Morgan, Leslie A. 1981: Economic Changes at midlife widowhood: A Longitudinal Analysis. *Journal of Marriage and the Family,* Vol. 43, No. 4, pp. 899-907.

Mukherjee, Prabhatil 1978: *Hindu Women—Normative Models,* New Delhi, Orient Langman Ltd.

Mulla, Dinshah Fardunji, 1960: *Principles of Hindu Law,* (2nd Edn.) Bombay: Tripathi Pvt. Ltd.

Mullati, Leela 1989: *The Bhakti Movement and the Status of Women: A Case Study of Virasaivism,* Abhinav Publications.

Nag, B.C. 1968: Hindus have fewer women, fewer brides and more widows, (*Organizer,* Vol. 21, No. 23.)

Nagesh, H.V. and Katti A.P. (Edn) 1988: *Widowhood in India.* Dharwad, SD-MET and JSS.

Nair, P.T. 1978: *Marriage and Dowry in India,* Calcutta, Minerva Associates.

Nair, Thankappan P. 1970: The First Hindu Widow Remarriage. *Bhavans Journal,* Vol. 17, pp. 39-41.

Nandimath, S.C. 1942: *A Handbook of Virasaivism,* Motilal Banarsidass.

Nand, Lokesh Chandra 1989: *Women in Delhi Sultinate,* Vohra Publishers and Distributors, Allahabad.

Nirmala Nandkumar 1987: Woidowhood in India Problems and Issues. Dharwad, Janata Shikshana Samiti, National Seminar on Widowhood in India.

Neera Desai, M. Krishnaraj, 1990: *Women and Society in India,* New Delhi, Ajanta Publications (India).

Ohio State University 1988: Sibling suport and Older Widow's Wellbeing. *Journal of Marriage and The Family,* Vol. 50, No. 1-6, p. 173.

Pakrasi, Kanti 1966: A Study of Widowhood in India, 1951. (*Bulletin of the Cultrual Research Institute,* Vol. 5, No. 1-3, pp. 67-74).

Paranjpye, Sai 1971: Home for Grandmothers. (Hingre Shikshan Sanstha Poona), (*The Hindustan Times,* pp. 67-74)

Parni, Sashanka Sekhar, 1975-76: Life of Widows in Gupta Period. (*Journal of Ancient Indian History,* Vol. 9, No. 1-2, pp. 79-96).

Paravathamma, C. 1972: *Sociological Essays in Veerashaivism,* Popular Prakashan, Bombay.

Pathare Record Association 1869: *Marriage of Hindu Widows,* Bombay, Indu Prakash Press.

Peterson, James A. and Briley Michaell 1977: *Widows and Widowhood—A Creative Approach to Being Alone,* Chicago, Association Press.

Phelps, H.A. 1983: *Contemparary Social Problems,* New York, Prentice hall.

Pimpley, P.N. 1964: Institutional Intergration of Action Elements, Intergration in conblict: A Sociological analysis, *Sociological Bulletin.*

Punwani, Jyoti 1971 (Aug.): Corollaries of Widowhood. (*Eve's Weekly,* pp. 41-42).

Pundita Ramabai Saraswati: 1888. 1984: *The High Caste Hindu Women,* New Delhi, Inter-India Publications.

Pratima Kumari 1988: *Changing Values Among Young Women,* Delhi, Amar Prakashan.

Rao, Ramana M.V. 1956: Century of Hindu Widow's

Remarriage Act. *Social Welfare,* Vol. Ill, No. 2, pp. 11-12.

Rajan, S. Irudaya (Mrs) 1987 (Mar): Widowhood and Remarriage among Roman Cathelics—An Evidence from the Ecclesiastical Registers. Dharwad, Janata Shikshana Samtis Ins.'tute of Economic Research, National Seminar on Widowhood in India.

Rajaretnam, T.E. Gandhi 1987: Socio-Economic and Demographic Aspects of widowhood in Athoor and Bathalagundu Blocks in Tamil Nadu, Dharwad, Janata Shikshana Samits Dharwad, National Seminar on Widowhood in India.

Rama Rao, G. And Mr. G. Rohini Devi. 1987 (Mar): Socio-Demographic Aspects of Widows (Selected States in India) Janata Sjhikshana Samitis Dharwad, National Seminar on widowhood in India.

Raghnandha Reddy, C. 1986: *Changing Status of Educated Working Women,* Delhi, B.R. Publishing Corporation.

Rogers, J.M. 1980: The newly widowed employee. (*Journal of Employment Counseling,* Vol. 17, No. 4, pp. 223-239.)

Rosow-Irwing 1967: *Social Integration of the Aged,* New York, The Free Press.

Roy Burman, B.K. 1970: Working paper on Sociology of National Integration: A Rapid Review on Concept and problems. Tenth All India Sociological Conference, Hyderabad.

Roy, Ajit Kumar 1985: *Widows are Not for Burning,* New Delhi, ABC Publishing House.

Sachchidananda and Sinha, Ramesh P. 1984: *Women's Rights: Myth and Reality,* Jaipur, Printwell Publishers.

Sadasivayya, T.M.H. 1978: *A Discourse on Veerashaivism,* Bombay—Bharatiya Vidya Bahavan.

Sadasivaiah, H.M. (Dr.) 1967: *A Comparative Study of Two Virasaiva Monasteries, Mysore,* Mysore University.

Shaikh, K.N 1968 (Feb.): Widowhood: A Great Social Problem. (*Mirror,* Vol. 7, No. 4, pp. 41-43).

Sharma, Vera 1977: Widowhood: Still a Curse? (*Eve's Weekly*, pp. 41-42).

Shivamurthy Shivacharya Mahaswamiji (Dr), 1990: Religion and Society At Cross-Roads, Sirigere (Citradurga, Dist) Sri Taralabalu Jagadguru Brihaman-math.

Shah, Kalpana 1984: *Women's liberation and Voluntary Action*, Delhi, Ajanta Publications.

Silverman, Phyllis Rilfe 1969: The Widow-to-Widow Programme—An Experiment in Preventive Intervention, *Mental Hygiene*, Vol. 53, No. 3, pp. 333-337.

Silverman, Phyllis Rolfe, 1979: The Widows as a Care giver in a program of preventive Intervention with Other Widow. *Mental Hygiene*, Vol. 54. No. 4, pp. 540-547.

Singh, Gurmeet M.P. and Mill, Sukhdeep 1986 April: Problems of Widowhood, *Indian Journal of Social Work*, Vol. XLVII, No. 1.

Shri Kumar Swamiji 1960: *Virashaiva Philosophy and Mysticism*, Dharwar, Shri. V.R. Koppal. M.A.B.T., Navakalyana Math.

Singh, Gurmeet M.P. 1988: Restraints to widow remarriage, *Social Changes*, Vol. 18; No.3.

Singh, T.R. 1969: Widow Remarriage Among Brahamans—A Sociological Study, *The Eastern Anthropologist*. Vol. 22, No. 1, pp. 75-87.

Singh, Vasta Rajendra 1976: The Remarriage and Rehabilitation of the Hindu Widows in India, 1856-1914. *Journal of Indian History*, Vol. 54, No. 3, pp. 713-730.

Sakhare, M.R. 1978: The History and Philosophy of Lingayat Religion, Dharwad, C.S. Kanavi Director, Extension Service and Publications, Karanataka University.

Sandra, Byford Wake, Michael J. Sporakowski 1972 (Feb): An Intergenerational Comparison of Attitudes Towards Supporting Aged parents, *Journal of Marriage and Family*, Vol. 34, No. 1.

Sapru, R.K. 1989: *Women and Development,* New Delhi, Ashok Publishing House.

Sargeant, N.C. 1963: *The Lingayats,* Christian Institute for the study of Religion and Society, Bangalore.

Sinha, R.K. and Tara Kanitkar 1987: Marital Discolution in India, Dharwad Janata Shikshan Samiti, National Seminar on Widowhood in India.

Singh Kulwant 1986: *Hindu Women's Right to Property in India,* New Delhi, Deep and Deep Publications.

Shrut, Samuel D. 1958: Attitudes Towards Old Age and Death, *Mental Hygiene,* Vol. 42, No. 2, pp. 259-266.

Smith, Ken R., Cathleen D. Zick 1986 (Aug): The Incidence of proverty among the Recently Widowhood Mediating Factors in the life course. *Journal of Marriage and the Family,* Vol. 48.

Stroebe, M.S. and W. Stroebe 1983: Who suffers more? Sex difference in health risks of the widowed. *Psychological Bulletin,* Vol. 93, No. 2.

Shyam Lal, 1972 (Sept.): Some Characterstics of the widows in rural society. (*Rural India,* Vol. 35, No. 9, pp. 205-08).

Subramanyan, Y.K. 1973: Widow in our Society. (*The Hindustan Times,* pp. 7:3.)

Sudhir Chandra, 1985: Widow Remarriage and Later Nineteenth Century. Indian Literature, (for private circulation only).

Sweet, James 1972: The living arrangement of seperated Widowed and divorced mothers. (*Demography,* Vol. 9, No. 1.)

Syamala, M. 1987: Here Widows are Actually Worshipped. *Eve's Weekly.* (Aug., 8-14).

Talcott Persons: *The Social System,* New Delhi, Amerinal Publishing Co. Pvt Ltd.

Tapper, Druce Elliot 1979: Widows and Goddesses; Female roles in diety symbolism in a South Indian Village. (*Contribution to Indian Sociology,* Vol. 13, No. 1, pp. 1-31).

Thomas, F.O. Dea 1969: *The Sociology of Religion,* Prentice, Hall of India Pvt Ltd., New Delhi.

Tripathi, B.D. 1977: *Nature of Sociological Theories the Action Approach,* New Delhi, Sterling Publishers Pvt. Ltd.

Toth Andre and Toth Susan 1980: Group Work With Widows *Social Work,* Vol. 25, No. 1, pp. 63-65.

(The) Widow in our Society *(The Hindustan Times,* 6 Jan 1973, p. 7:3).

Veerasalingam, K. 1970: The First Widow Marriage. *Triveni,* Vol. 39, No. 3, pp. 48-54.

Vidyasagar, I.C. 1976: *Marriage of Hindu Widows,* Calcutta, K.P. Bagchi and Co.

Vanaja Dhruwarajan 1989: *Hindu Women and the Power of Ideology,* New Delhi, Vistaar Publications.

Vinick, B.V. 1978: Remarriage in Old Age, *The Family Coordinator,* Vol. 27, No. 3, pp. 359-363.

Vohra, R.N. 1972: Women in Vedic India, *Social Welfare.* Vol. XIX. No. 7.

Whyte, Robert Orr, Whyte Pauline 1982: *The Women of Rural Asia.*

Weiss, Robert S. 1984 (Feb): The Impact of Marital Dissulation on income and Consumption in single-parent Households. *Journal of Marriage and Family.*

Wilkinson, T.S. (Dr.) and Bhandarkar P.L. (Dr.) 1977: *Methodology and Techniques of Social Research,* Bombay, Himalaya Publishing House.

William, P. Scott 1988: *Dictionary of Sociology,* New Delhi, Goyal Saab Publishers and Distributors.

William, Skidmore, 1987: *Theoretical thinking in Sociology,* Cambridge, Cambridge University Press, Cambridge.

Wamble, Dale 1966: *Foundations for Marriage and Family Relations,* New York, Macmillan.

Widows are the Silent Sufferers. (*Yojana.* 16 June 1978, pp. 27-30).

Worse than Sati: (*Indian Express,* 22 Dec 1976, pp. 4-1).

Young, Michael, Benjamin Bernard and Wallis, Chirs 1963:

The Mortality of Widowers. *The Lancet*, Vol. II, No. 1, pp. 42-44.

Zink, Cathleen D. and Ken R. Smith 1988 (Feb): Recent Widowhood, Remarriage and changes in Economic well being, *Journal of Marriage and the Family*, Vol. 50. No. 1, pp. 233-244.

Zilboorg, Gregory 1943: Fear of Death. *The Psychoanalytic Quarterly*, Vol. 12, No. 1, pp. 465-475.

Thesis and Dissertations

Bansal Vimal 1979: Widows-Murauna Ph.D. Thesis, ICSSR Library, New Delhi.

Baidyanath, Saraswati 1983: The Kashivasi Widows, ICSSR Research Project Report, New Delhi.

Dhumatkar, M.G. 1928: Position of Hindu Women with Special Reference to Maharasthtra, Ph.D. Thesis, Bombay University.

Gupta, Mira: Status and role of Hindu widows a sociological study of 400 widows in the city of Lucknow. Ph.D. Thesis, Lucknow University.

Hate, C.A. 1946: *The Social position of Hindu Widows*, Ph.D. Thesis. Bombay University, Bombay.

Jambagi Sulochana 1964: Life and Activities of Lingayat Widows, M.A. Dissertation, Karanatak University, Dharwad.

Kitchlu, T.N. 1982: A Study of Socio-economic Condition of Widows in Union Territory of Delhi, Project Report. Dept. of Social Work, University of Delhi, Delhi.

Kaur, Sharanjit 1974: Social Adjustment of War Widows M.A. Dissertation. Punjab University, Chandigarh.

Katti, A.P. and Nagesh, H.V. 1984: A Socio-Economic Study of Widows (in Hubli City and Neighbouring Villages)—A Project Report, JSS Institute of Economic Research, Dharwad.

Mehta, Vatsala 1958: The Hindu Widow With Special Reference to Gujrat, M.A. Dissertation, Bombay University, Bombay.

Nagesh, H.V. and Katti, A.P. 1983: A Study of Widows—A Project Report, JSS Istitute of Economic Research, Dharwad.

Patil, Godavari: Widowhood: A State of Deprivation, Ph.D. Thesis, Karnataka University, Dharwad.

Sudha, S.S. 1979: A Study of Jangam Community in Davangere, Mysore, Dissertation submitted for M.A. degree of Mysore University.

Census and Official Reports

Census of India, 1951-1991.

Karnataka State Gazetteer, Part-142. Kamat, Suryanath. (Ed). 1982. Government of Karnatak, Bangalore.

Mysore state Gazetteer - Gulbarga district, B.N. Sathyan B.A. (Hons.), Bangalore.

Census of Gulbarga District, 1991.

Index

■■■